Painted

APPLIQUÉ

A NEW APPROACH

Linda M. Poole

American Quilter's Society

P.O. Box 3290 • Paducah, KY 42002-3290
Fax 270-898-1173 • e-mail: orders@AQSquilt.com

Located in Paducah, Kentucky, the American Quilter's Society (AQS) is dedicated to promoting the accomplishments of today's quilters. Through its publications and events, AQS strives to honor today's quiltmakers and their work and to inspire future creativity and innovation in quiltmaking.

Executive Book Editor: Elaine Brelsford
Book Editor: Kathy Davis
Proofreader: Joann Treece
Graphic Design: Lynda Smith
Cover Design: Michael Buckingham
Quilt Photography: Charles R. Lynch

Additional copies of this book may be ordered from the American Quilter's Society, PO Box 3290, Paducah, KY 42002-3290, or online at www.AmericanQuilter.com.

Text © 2013, Author, Linda M. Poole
Artwork © 2013, American Quilter's Society

American Quilter's Society
P.O. Box 3290 • Paducah, KY 42002-3290
Fax 270-898-1173 • e-mail: orders@AQSquilt.com

Library of Congress Cataloging-in-Publication Data

Poole, Linda M.
    Painted appliqué : a new approach / Linda M. Poole.
      pages cm
    ISBN 978-1-60460-109-1
    1. Appliqué. 2. Textile painting. I. Title.
    TT779.P665 2013
    746.44'5--dc23
                                    2013044822

Dedication & Acknowledgments

Heartfelt love and appreciation go to my mom and dad, Gloria and Gero, who nurtured my love for art, travel, photography, and needlework throughout my life—you always believed in me. You are the best parents a daughter could have. You never batted an eye when I said I wanted to be an artist when I grew up. How lucky I am!

To my husband, Ray, the love and light in my life—you keep me balanced, laughing, and hugged. You inspire me every day with your positive spirit. I love you!

To my best friend and mischievous prank-loving counterpart, Billie Jo Rosado, who brings out the best in me—I call her my sister. She knows I work best under pressure and she kept reminding me of that.

To my little Corgi pup, Zoie—you make me smile every day and made me realize that life isn't always about work but about throwing Frisbees, too.

To my dear friends who have been by my side while walking this path of wild, uncharted creativity-gone-wild—your humor kept me sane.

I want to express infinite gratitude and appreciation to:

My dear friend, Debbie Caffrey, who generously volunteered her vacation and family time to pre-edit this book. Her left-side brain "wordsmithed" my right-side brain's words into text that anyone can understand. She encouraged me every step of the way.

Charlotte Angotti who talked me off the creative block ledge numerous times, always telling me, "You can do it!"

Laura Orben, Linda J. Hahn, Joan Shay, and Mickey Depre who checked on me to see how I was doing and to make sure that I got outside away from the sewing machine and computer.

Gloria Grohs, Helen Umstead, and Laura Heine, the ladies who helped me sew bindings, block quilts, and meet my deadline.

Sherry Rogers-Harrison, Lisa Sipes, Pamela Joy Dransfeldt, and Karen McTavish for quilting some of the projects.

The Milford Valley Quilters Guild of Milford, Pennsylvania, my quilt guild, where it all began with the camaraderie of quilt lovers, friendships, and great food. You inspire me!

Thank you, Bonnie McCaffery, for your amazing talent of photography and for taking my author photo.

The staff of AQS has always been generous and understanding. They treat me like family.

The companies who sent products to me: InkFusion™ and PaintFusion™ Aurifil™ Thread; Pellon®, RK Distributing for Floriani Stitch N Wash Fusible® Stabilizer, Stella Lighting, and The Warm™ Company.

Contents

Introduction

Every quilt is a piece of art.

Appliqué has a magical way of satisfying the inner artist in us. Fabric is the paint, the pattern is the canvas, and the threaded needle is our paintbrush. It is an exciting experience knowing that each stitch we take will bring us closer to the completion of our masterpiece.

What if we were to combine the artistry of appliqué and painting? Are you intrigued? Using a flower for an example, we no longer need to cut out individual petals and sew them back together. Instead, imagine if our flower could be cut out as one big unit and the petals painted. The best part is that we still get to sew the appliqué unit to the background or to another piece.

In this book I will teach you how paints, mediums, and ink pencils work on fabric. Fabric markers and Gelly Roll® pens add touches of whimsy. To make your appliqués, complete instructions with photos are provided in each pattern.

Play, experiment, and above all, be that artist you have inside you.

We keep moving forward, opening new doors, and doing new things because we're curious, and curiosity keeps leading us down new paths.

Walt Disney

Materials & Supplies

Freezer paper is found at the grocery store. One side is paper and the other side has a shiny plastic coating that, when ironed, temporarily adheres to your fabrics. If you iron it to a section of fabric and you change your mind about the placement, you can peel it up and re-iron it in another place. You can purchase freezer paper that is already cut to size for printing patterns from your computer on your ink-jet printer.

Fusible water-soluble stabilizers are used the same way as freezer paper in the techniques throughout this book. They are sheer enough to see through when tracing patterns. Patterns can be printed on the sheets with your inkjet printer. This stabilizer is made of half soluble and half nonsoluble fibers. When finished appliquéing all of the pieces to the background, immerse the quilt top in water to remove the stabilizer. One layer of soluble materials will dissolve and the nonsoluble fibers will remain for stability, while the fabric remains soft. One benefit is that there is no need to cut the background fabric behind the appliqué, if you so choose. Many times, I just leave the stabilizer inside without rinsing.

Water-soluble glue sticks are found in office supply stores. Elmer's® Washable School Glue Stick is my preferred glue stick. When first applied it is purple and disappears when dry. UHU® Glue Stick is another wonderful product.

Toothpicks or skewers help turn and smooth out any inconsistencies as you turn over your appliqué edges. My favorite toothpick is found at the Cracker Barrel® Old Country Store checkout counters. They are sturdy and have a flat head on the top.

For fusible bias tape, use a **bias tape maker**. They come in a variety of sizes to make bias tape from ¼" to 2" wide.

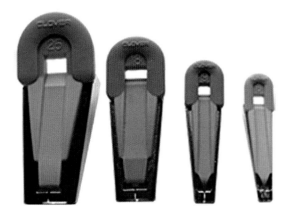

Teflon® pressing sheets will protect your ironing board from fusible materials. The professional grade sheet I use withstands heat up to 600 degrees. Nothing sticks to it, and after using it, I can quickly wipe it with a damp cloth and roll it for storage. I also use it to protect a painted area when I press it.

Light boxes or windows are helpful when you need a light source behind your pattern to trace it. If you do not have a light box, you can make a substitute by resting a piece of tempered glass between two tables and setting a lamp underneath the glass. My favorite method is to tape fabric, freezer paper, or fusible water-soluble stabilizer to a clean window, slip the pattern underneath, and trace.

Permanent pens and markers add accents on painted areas of your appliqué, whether they are small details or outlines. When looking for a marking pen, make sure it will work on fabric, is waterproof, and will not bleed. Try the pen on fabrics that already have paints and a fabric medium applied to them. You want pens that do not skip and that last a long time so you won't run out of ink in the middle of detailing an area.

IDenti®-pen comes in many colors. It has two tips. One end is a fine point and the other end has a fine bullet-shaped fiber tip. It is permanent, waterproof, fade resistant, and has low odor.

Prismacolor Premier® Brush Tip Markers also come in lots of colors. Use them to draw thick, fine, or varied lines with one stroke. They move over the painted areas smoothly.

IDenti-pen, Prismacolor markers, and **Tsukineko® Fabrico Markers** all have a dual tip. The ink is permanent and does not need to be set with heat. One end of the marker has a brush tip to fill in larger areas and the other end has a bullet tip for finer detail work.

Jacquard® Tee Juice™ medium-point markers come in a variety of colors. They are acid free, archival, lightfast, washable, and dry-cleanable. They must be heat-set with an iron when used on fabric.

Pentel® Gel Roller for Fabric is a no-smudge, no-smear ink that is permanent on most fabrics. The water-based pigment ink withstands repeated washings.

Tulip® Fabric Markers are best used on white and light-colored fabrics or to add accents to already painted fabrics. They come in a wide array of colors.

Your choices of markers are plentiful. Visit your favorite craft store, quilt shop, or online store. Read what each brand does and decide what is right for you. Keep in mind, if you plan to wash your quilt or displaying it in direct sun, make sure the inks are fade resistant and waterproof.

I like to store all my markers and pens horizontally to insure they do not dry out.

Derwent Inktense water-soluble ink pencils come in packages of assorted colors, or you can purchase individual ink pencils in open stock. The colors are vibrant. Blending two or more together produces even more beautiful colors.

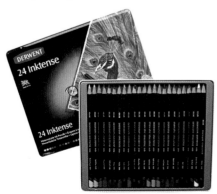

There are two ways to use the ink pencils. One is coloring your fabric with the dry pencil as if you are coloring in a coloring book. Pressing the pencil lightly gives you a soft color. Applying more pressure will make the colors stronger. You must paint over your coloring with a fabric medium to bring the ink to life and make it permanent on fabric.

The second way to use these ink pencils is to dip your paintbrush into a fabric medium and brush over the tip of the pencil. The tip of the pencil becomes wet and the ink comes off onto your brush tip. Simply brush it on your fabric.

If your pencil breaks while coloring or sharpening the pencil, save the point in a little jar. You can load your brush with fabric medium and brush off the color from the broken point.

When I want to lift just a little bit of color for an accent, I dip a paintbrush into InkFusion fabric medium and rub the brush on the InkTense ink pencil tip to activate the color.

Make a color reference key. This will help you decide on colors when painting your appliqué. Iron freezer paper to the back of a piece of white fabric. Draw squares with a pencil and color each with a different color. Paint fabric medium over the colored squares. Write the color name next to the square.

Blend two colors together to see the new color it will make. Make a key for the new blended color.

Dry pigment paints can be added to textile paints or mixed with InkFusion.

Dry pigment is ground into a fine powder and mixed with a binder to make paint. The binder is called fabric medium. The intensity of the color depends on the amount of pigment you add to the fabric medium.

Another way to use dry pigments is to dip your brush in a fabric medium and then dip the loaded brush into a little bit of the dry pigment.

Dry pigments come in a wide assortment of colors. Be very careful when mixing dry pigments and fabric medium. One

sneeze or a breeze can send the powder everywhere. I suggest opening the jar in a shoe box top to avoid spilling powders on your project or work surface. Keep the jar of pigments in the shoe box top while adding it to your fabric medium.

Textile paint can be used straight from the bottle. Stir it thoroughly. Textile paint sits on the surface of the fabric fibers. Transparent paints are suitable for white or lightly-colored fabrics. Use opaque paints to cover color or pattern that is already on the fabric. Pearlescent paints have a beautiful iridescent sheen. Colors can be mixed.

Read the label to see if the painted fabric needs to be heat set. Air dry painted fabrics before heat setting. Many do not require heat setting, but I always do.

Jacquard® textile paints glide smoothly onto fabric when you are painting small or large areas. The painted fabric becomes washable and dry-cleanable when set with a hot iron or dryer, and it remains flexible and soft.

PRO® Chemical & Dye PROfab Textile Paints are water-based pigments that have a Jello-like consistency. Mix these paints with **PROfab base extender** to create pastel shades and with PROfab Lo Crock for watercolor effects. Heat setting is necessary to make the paint permanent. The colors can be mixed to create a larger palette of colors.

Liquitex® Soft Body paints are the most permanent paints for fabrics. They offer exceptional quality, durability, adhesion, and the largest assortment of pure pigments of any professional quality acrylic paint. Adjust the paint to the desired consistency using Liquitex fabric mediums. I like to add **InkTense** to it for an extra glimmer. Heat setting, steaming, or chemical fixing is not required.

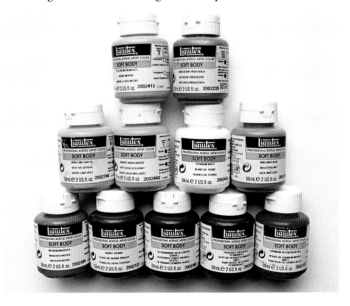

Fabric medium is a thick opaque fluid when it is wet but dries clear. It slows down the drying time of the paint in order to have more time to blend and paint on the fabric. It keeps fabric soft after it has been painted, and makes paint permanent and washable. It prevents bleeding, cracking, or fading of the color. Experiment with the proportions of medium and paint you blend together. The more medium you add the more transparent the paint will become. Start with a 1:1 ratio.

There are many brands of medium. I particularly love **PaintFusion™** and **InkFusion™**. InkFusion is iridescent, having a silver or gold tint to it. Other fabric mediums have an iridescence to them, as well. Add fabric medium to watercolor pencils and **Derwent Inktense Ink Pencils**. Fabric crayons and fabric gels can be painted over with fabric medium.

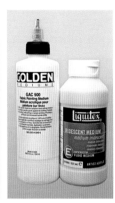

| PaintFusion medium | InkFusion medium | Golden and Liquitex medium |

Fabrics used for painting must be of good quality and have a high thread count. Use 100% white cotton fabric and prewash in hot water to remove any sizing so the paint adheres well. PFD (prepared for dye) is another wonderful choice, as it has no optical whiteners, chemicals, or sizing.

When ironing painted fabric, make sure it is completely dry before ironing it. Twenty-four hours is the optimal time to let the piece cure before ironing.

To set your fabric paints, turn the iron to medium-hot with no steam. Start by ironing the wrong side of the fabric for 3–5 minutes. Keep moving the iron over the area. Turn the fabric over and place a pressing cloth or Teflon sheet over the painted area. Press again.

Brushes: Walking through the paintbrush aisle of an art supply or craft store can be daunting. Every shape, length, and style will be in front of you. The first thing to do is run your fingers over the bristles. See if the bristles separate easily and continue to hold their shape. Make sure the bristles are not loose or falling out. There is nothing worse than having to pick out bristles that have fallen out onto the painted fabric.

Opt for a medium-priced brush if you are not sure what to get. Pick the brush up and see how it feels in your hand. I prefer **Loew-Cornell paintbrushes**. The brushes I used in this book's projects are: flat, filbert, shader, and round scrubber. The goal in fabric painting is to use a good brush that will marry the paints into the weave of the fabric, not just move the paint on top of the fabric.

A flat brush tip is used for filling wide spaces.

A filbert brush tip is used for blending and painting soft rounded edges.

A shader brush tip is used for curved strokes and filling corners. The tip of the bristles reaches into small areas.

A round brush tip is used for filling small areas. It is used to create fine to thick lines by asserting different amounts of pressure to the brush strokes.

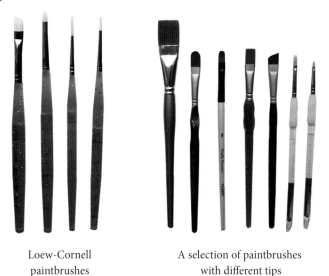

Loew-Cornell
paintbrushes

A selection of paintbrushes
with different tips

Caring for and Cleaning Paintbrushes

Do not leave a paintbrush in a container of water. The bristles will become frayed and bend, which is irreversible.

Swish the paintbrush in water and squeeze out excess water with a paper towel. Using hand soap or artist's

paintbrush soap, gently work it into the bristles with your fingers.

Hold the paintbrush under running lukewarm water. Squeeze out the excess water again with a paper towel. Let the paintbrushes dry horizontally.

If you have trouble finding any of the supplies above, see Resources on page 110.

Glue Stick Appliqué Technique

This is the appliqué method I like the best. All the appliqué pieces are sewn together before finally stitching the appliqué to the background fabric. Sections can be stored in little baggies, making for a very convenient travel project.

Supplies

Background fabric and fabric for the appliqué pieces.
    All fabrics should be prewashed and pressed.

Machine appliqué needles

Freezer paper or fusible water-soluble stabilizer sheets

Pencil, eraser, paper clips, stapler, and staple remover

Fine Sharpie® permanent black marker

Light box or window
    Water-soluble blue marker. The blue markings made by water-soluble markers must be removed with cold water.

Paper and fabric scissors

Water-soluble glue stick

Skewer or sturdy toothpick

Bodkin or tweezers

Iron and ironing surface

Small piece of lightweight cardboard

Warm water

Damp washcloth

Towel

Small baggies

Making a Master Copy

Some patterns have red lines on them. Those lines are to be used only in the painted appliqué versions. Ignore the red lines when making fabric appliqué templates.

Notice that the asymmetrical patterns are reversed relative to the quilts in the photos so that the appliqué templates will be reversed. These reversed templates, when placed on the wrong side of the fabrics, produce the correct orientation in the finished quilt.

Use a photocopier to enlarge designs to the desired size. If you like to work with small pieces, there is no need for you to enlarge the design. To make templates, tape the master copy to a window or light box. Tape a piece of freezer paper or fusible water-soluble stabilizer, shiny-side down, over the master copy. Trace the pattern on the dull side of the freezer paper or fusible water-soluble stabilizer with a pencil or fine black Sharpie permanent marker. Be sure to copy all the dots, numbers, and words. A light box or window is not necessary if you can see the design through the freezer paper or stabilizer.

Step :

1 Use scissors to cut the freezer paper or stabilizer template on the traced lines.

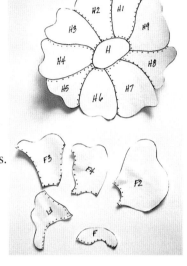

2 Iron the shiny side of the freezer paper or stabilizer to the wrong side of the fabric.

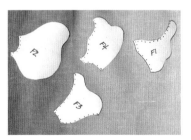

3 Trim around each template with your fabric scissors, leaving a scant ¼" seam allowance.

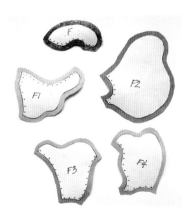

Tip : A closed area is one that must have the seam allowances turned over the freezer paper or stabilizer before being glue stick appliquéd. An open area does not need to be turned over because it will be covered by another piece. On the template patterns, you will see dots that indicate an open area. Just think of the dots as little Os for open.

4 Make little snips in the seam allowance around the curves where there are no dots. Cut almost to the freezer paper or stabilizer, stopping about a thread away.

5 Place a piece of cardboard under the pieces you are gluing to protect the work surface. Use a water-soluble glue stick to apply a line of glue on the seam allowance where there are no dots.

6 Use a damp washcloth to wipe your fingers clean of any glue residue. I store my damp washcloth in a baggie and keep it nearby.

With the inside of your thumb, fold the glued seam allowance over the freezer paper or stabilizer.

7 A toothpick or skewer will help smooth the curved edges or pull in unruly fabric.

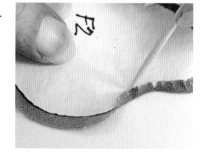

Overlapping Pieces

Look carefully at each design to determine which pieces will overlap one another.

8 Glue the top raw-edge seam allowance of one piece and attach to its corresponding piece. Use the master pattern to make sure they fit together perfectly. Appliqué the pieces together.

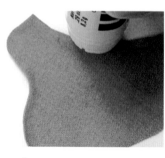

9 Hold the pieces up to a window or light so you can see exactly how the raw edge and the glued turned over edge will fit together. It is like fitting puzzle pieces together! Hand or machine appliqué together.

Making Multiple Pieces

Step :

1 Place the shiny side of the freezer paper or stabilizer on top of the master pattern and trace one or two leaves on the dull side with a pencil.

2 Cut a rough square around the leaves. Cut more squares of freezer paper or stabilizer the same size.

3 Stack the squares, making sure the dull side of the sheets is facing up. The square with the traced leaves should be on top.

4 Staple through the stack of sheets.

5 Cut out the stacks of leaves.

6 Remove the staples with a staple remover.

7 When you have multiples of a piece, paper clip them together to keep them organized.

Sharp Points

Apply glue to the tips of the seam allowance on the wrong side of the fabric. Fold the points down. Apply glue to the seam allowance at the left of the points and fold over. Repeat for the opposite side.

Preparing the Background

Step :

1 Cut a piece of background fabric an inch or two larger than the size needed for the project. The patterns in this book allow for one inch in each direction. The instructions at the end of the pattern tell you what size to trim the background.

2 Tape the master copy, pattern-side up, to a light box or window.

3 Center the background fabric, right-side up, on the pattern. Tape the fabric to the light box or window. With a water-soluble blue marker, lightly trace the pattern onto the fabric. This tracing is the placement guide for the appliquéd units; therefore, you need not mark every detail.

4 Using the traced lines on the background fabric for reference, appliqué the units to the background.

Removing the Fusible Layer of the Fusible Water-Soluble Stabilizer

Step :

1 After the final appliqué has been sewn to the background, use a bucket of water and a clean sponge or rag and slowly dab the piece in sections on the back of the quilt top. Leave for about 15 minutes to dissolve the fusible. There will still be a thin layer of fusible inside the appliqué. It acts as a stabilizer and is soft to the hand. It is not necessary to cut away the background fabric.

2 Roll the piece in a thick towel to remove more water. Gently press the appliqué with steam on a dry towel.

Removing the Freezer Paper

Step :

1 After the final appliqué has been sewn to the background, trim the background fabric from behind the appliqués, leaving ¼" for seam allowance.

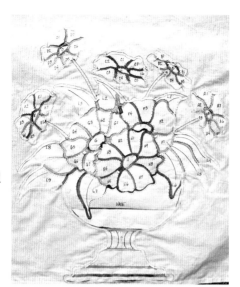

2 Soak the entire piece in lukewarm water and agitate slowly with your hand, or use a bucket of water and a clean sponge or rag and slowly dab the piece in sections to loosen the freezer paper. Leave for about 15 minutes to dissolve the glue from the glue stick.

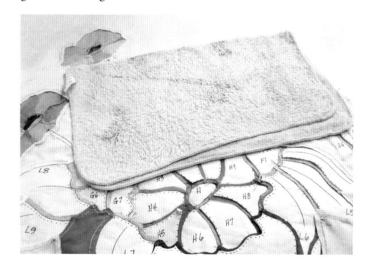

3 Gently remove the loose freezer paper with a bodkin, tweezers, or your fingers. Drain the used water and refill a sink with clean water. Dip the piece in clean water.

4 Gently squeeze out the excess water by hand.

5 Roll the piece in a thick towel to remove more water. Gently press the appliqué with steam on a dry towel.

Painted Appliqué Techniques

Painted appliqué uses the same basic instructions as the Glue Stick Appliqué Technique with a few exceptions. The biggest difference is that the outside edge of the design is traced on freezer paper or fusible water-soluble stabilizer sheets and cut out as a whole unit instead of cutting separate pieces.

Supplies

- PFD (prepared for dyeing) or white, tightly woven 100% cotton fabric – prewashed and pressed
- Freezer paper or fusible water-soluble stabilizer sheets
- Pencil and eraser
- Machine appliqué needles, fabric, and paper scissors
- Light box or window
- Water-soluble glue stick
- Skewer or sturdy toothpick
- Iron and ironing surface
- Small piece of lightweight cardboard
- Damp washcloth, paper towels, and a container with water
- Plastic to cover the work area
- Paintbrushes, textile paints, fabric markers, and fabric medium
- Masking tape, mixing cups, or small containers

Technique 1

Step :

1 Place the shiny side of the freezer paper or stabilizer on top of the reversed master pattern. Use a pencil to trace the entire design, the red lines and the black lines, on the dull side of the freezer paper or stabilizer.

2 Cut on the lines along the outside edge, leaving the entire design intact. Do not cut the individual pieces.

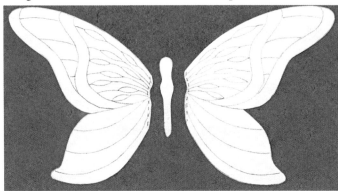

3 Iron the shiny side of the freezer paper or stabilizer to the PFD or white cotton fabric. With the fabric side on top, use a light source and lightly pencil in the inside lines on the fabric. Do not trace the outside edges of the appliqué.

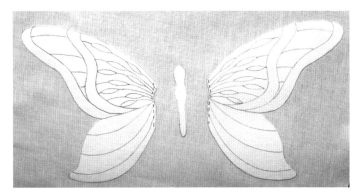

4 Trim the excess fabric, leaving a scant ¼" for seam allowance. Clip, glue, and turn over the seam allowances as directed for the Glue Stick Appliqué Technique on pages 11–13. Paint the appliqué as directed for the specific pattern. Gently press the appliqué with steam on a dry towel.

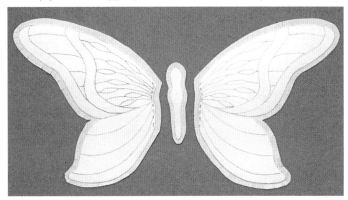

Technique 2

Step :

1 Place the PFD or white cotton fabric on top of the pattern and tape down. With a pencil, lightly trace the entire design on the fabric. Trace all lines.

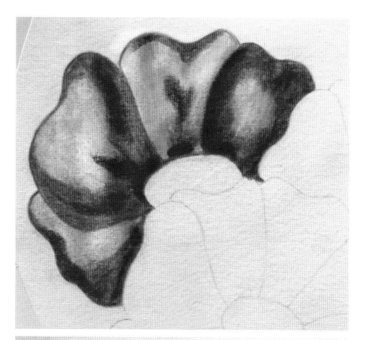

2 Iron a piece of freezer paper on the back of the fabric. It will stabilize the fabric while coloring and painting. Use a pencil to draw an arrow in a blank area outside of the traced pattern to define the top of the design. Paint the appliqué as directed in the pattern.

Allow the painted areas to dry. Peel off the freezer paper used to stabilize the fabric while painting.

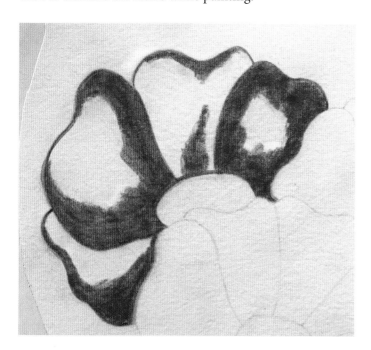

3 Turn the master pattern face down and tape it to a window or light box. Place a water-soluble stabilizer sheet, shiny-side down over the master pattern, and trace it with a pencil. Carefully cut around the outside edge of the traced pattern.

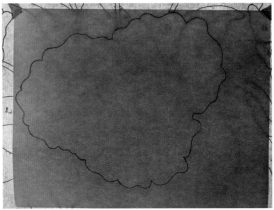

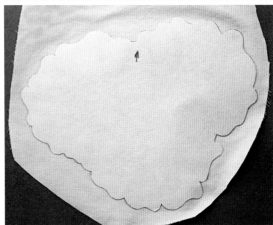

4 Iron the shiny side of the stabilizer to the wrong side of the painted appliqué. A light source is helpful to make sure the placement is perfect. Trim the excess fabric, leaving a scant ¼" for seam allowance. Clip, glue, and turn over the seam allowances as directed for the Glue Stick Appliqué Technique on pages 11–13.

Technique 3

Here is another way to bring designs to life:

Step :

1 Trace the pattern lines on PFD or white cotton fabric with a pencil. Iron freezer paper to the wrong side of the fabric to stabilize it while painting.

2 Brush a different color of paint in each section. Add a small amount of white textile paint to soften the colors.

3 Let the piece dry thoroughly and then iron with a pressing cloth or Teflon sheet over it for protection.

4 Proceed with appliqué instructions.

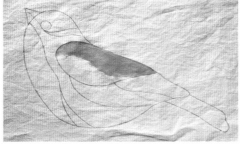

Do you realize that you just painted a wholecloth fabric ready to be quilted? You did! If you decide not to appliqué your painted piece, sandwich the wholecloth with batting and backing and quilt away! Bind to finish!

Making Circles & Ovals

Appliqué looks lovely when set into an oval or a circle. Your eyes go directly to the center of the appliqué showing all the beauty and detail in the work. Give it a try! You may never go back to the traditional setting of sewing an appliqué onto a square or rectangle again.

Circles

Step:

1 Decide on the size of the circle. A plate, pizza pan, or anything circular works well for a template. Another tool I like to use is a yardstick compass to draw circles.

2 Draw a circle on the smooth side of lightweight fusible interfacing. The interfacing has a slightly bumpy side, which is the fusible side that goes face down on the right side of the finished appliqué or the right side of the fabric.

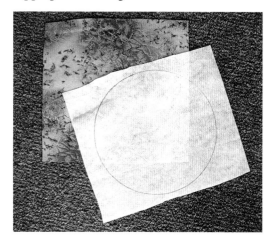

3 Center the circle over the appliqué or fabric. Press lightly, gently, and quickly in random spots with an iron (no steam)—just enough to tack it into place.

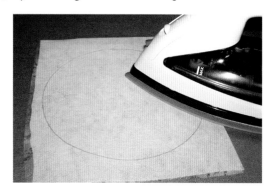

4 Sew completely around the circle on the pencil line and trim the seam allowances to ¼".

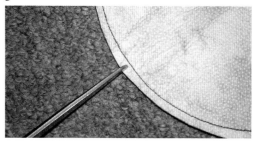

5 Cut slits in the seam allowance all around the circle's edge, stopping about one thread away from the machine stitching.

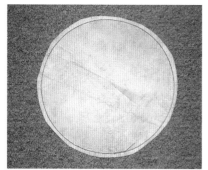

6 Cut a slit into the interfacing. Turn the piece right-side out by reaching inside the circle and pulling the fabric through the slit.

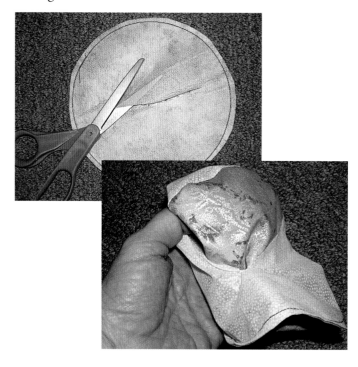

7 Slide a point turner or seam-creasing tool into the slit and smooth out the seam. Fuse the circle to another piece of fabric. Press the circle down with an iron (no steam). Appliqué the edge of the circle to the background fabric.

Ovals

Step :

1 Drawing ovals is easier than you might imagine. First, decide how long and wide the oval should be. Cut a strip of lightweight cardboard or template plastic that is an inch or two longer than half the oval's length and about 1" wide. This strip will be become the "ruler."

Mark an A near the left end of the ruler. Then add B and C, as follows: The distance between A and C is half the length of the desired oval. The distance between B and C is half its width.

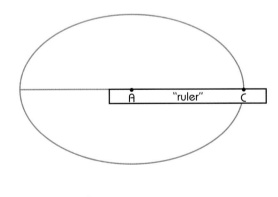

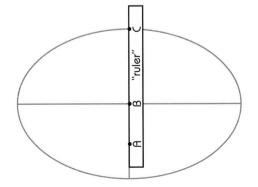

2 In the middle of a piece of paper, large enough to accommodate the oval, draw a line the length of the desired oval. At the center of the line, draw another line perpendicular to the first line for the oval's width.

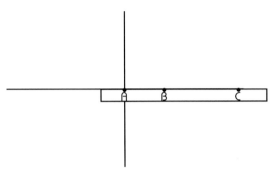

3 Align the ruler and place a mark on the paper at C. Move the A mark a short way down the vertical line and adjust B along the horizontal line. Make another mark at C.

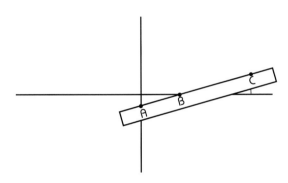

4 Keeping A on the vertical line and B on the horizontal line, continue moving the ruler short distances and marking the oval at C.

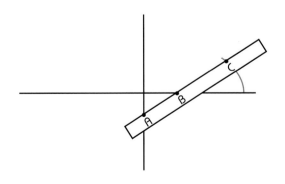

5 When A, B, and C are aligned on the vertical line, you will have marked one quarter of the oval. Repeat the marking instructions for each quarter to complete the oval.

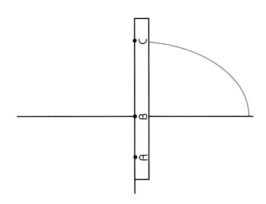

Alternatively, an oval can be made by folding a sheet of paper into quarters and using the ruler to draw one quarter of the oval on the folded sheet. Cut the folded paper on the line and unfold it to reveal the completed oval.

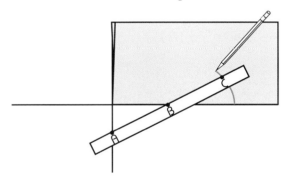

Trimming a Circle or Oval

Step :

1 Adding trim to circles or ovals adds a spark of fun to quilts. Fusible bias tape can be easily braided. Pin three pieces of bias tape together on a Teflon sheet on top of an ironing surface. Braid a few inches and iron to fuse it on the Teflon sheet. Braid and iron as much trim as is needed to go around the circle or oval.

2 When the braid has cooled, remove it from the Teflon sheet. Iron it around the circle or oval.

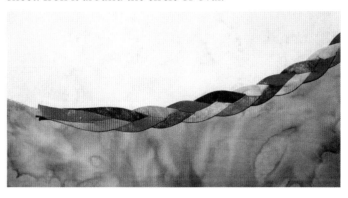

3 Machine stitch to hold it down.

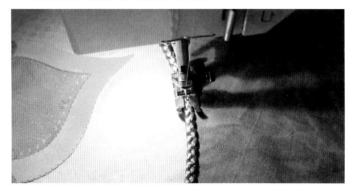

Purchased trims also work nicely. Look for those that will complement your work.

Tip : Long shoelaces are perfect for measuring around ovals and circles, telling you exactly how much trim you need. Gently bend and walk the lace around the shape until you get back to where you started. Mark the ending point on the shoelace. Measure the distance to that point. Add an inch or two for safety.

Making Bias Tape

Step :

1 Place the straight grain of the fabric over the 45 degree line on a cutting mat. Place a ruler on the fabric, aligning it with the 45 degree line.

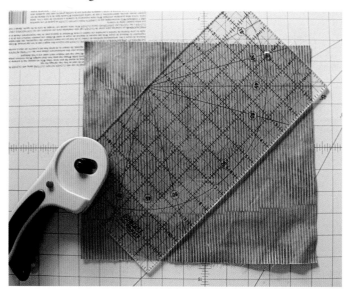

2 Use a rotary cutter and cut on the line.

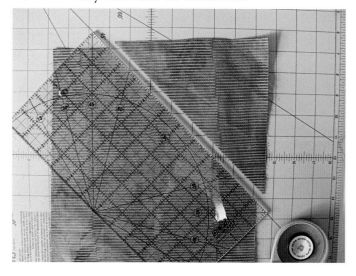

3 Measure from the trimmed edge and cut a bias strip ½" wider than the desired finished size of the bias tape.

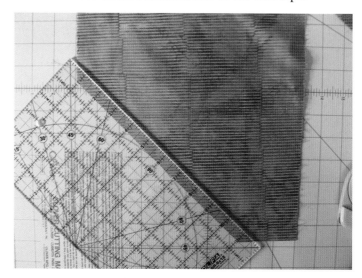

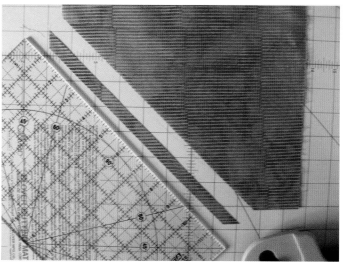

Tip : If you are not going to use fusible tape, spray the bias strip lightly with starch to hold the crease. If you are using fusible tape, do not use starch.

4 Bending the end of the bias strip in half will allow it to feed into the bias tape maker more easily. Turn the bias strip wrong-side up. With the metal side of the bias tape maker on top, feed the bent end of the strip into the opening.

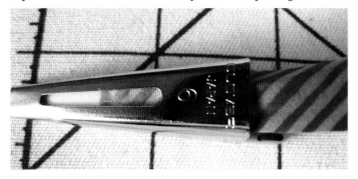

5 Use a pin, scissors tip, or another sharp object to gently push the bias tape through the bias tape maker until just a little bit of the tape comes out of the opening. You will be able to see the right side of the fabric through the slot on top.

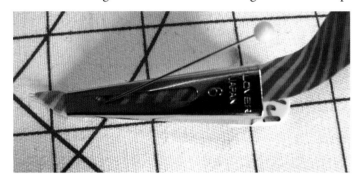

6 Turn the bias tape maker over and slip the fusible tape sticky-side down through the top slot. Gently pull the tape down to the bottom.

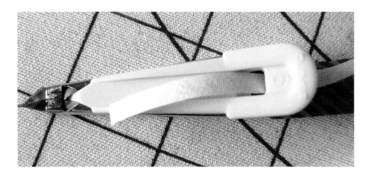

7 With the end of a hot iron (no steam), tap the fusible tape and the end of the bias strip together. Pin the end of the fabric strip to the ironing surface. Gently pull the bias tape

maker back while you follow close to the edge to iron the fusible to the bias tape.

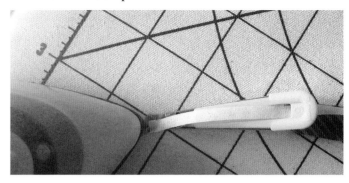

8 Move the pin as you iron more fusible bias tape to keep the strip straight. Keep the iron perpendicular to the horizontal strip while pulling and ironing.

9 Let the bias tape cool. Gently peel off the paper release strip. The bias tape is ready to be ironed into place and sewn.

Sewing the Bias Tape in Place

Fun choices for sewing the bias tape in place await you. Sewing machine decorative stitches, top stitching with a straight stitch, hand or machine appliqué, hand embroidery stitches, and using the twin needle on the sewing machine are just a few.

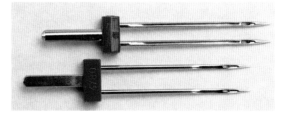

Tip : Do you want to make ⅛" bias tape? Make the traditional ¼" bias tape. Once it has cooled and the creases are set, run a glue stick along one seam allowance on the wrong side. Fold the tape in half. Glue and stitch it as you would wider bias tape.

Machine Appliqué

Supplies

Thread

Have you seen all the threads that are available? Today, we can choose cotton threads from an infinite range of colors and shades and from rainbows of variegated colors. We can select invisible threads that come in clear and smoke.

If you choose to use cotton thread, select one that closely matches the appliqué fabric. Use a fine 50/2 thread to help the threads sink into the appliqué when machine stitching.

Using monofilament thread shows no stitches! It also sinks nicely into the appliqués. Do your homework to make sure the monofilament thread is heat resistant. My favorites are Aurifil and Superior. See Resources on page 110.

I use monofilament in the bobbin, too. I wind the bobbin half full. You can also use a lightweight 50/2 thread in the bobbin when using monofilament in the needle.

Needles

A universal 70/10 needle does the job for invisible machine appliqué. Always replace the needle when starting a new project. You do not want the stitches to have large holes piercing the fabric because of an old needle. If the thread is shredding, if the stitches become uneven, or if the machine is making a banging sound, you need a new needle.

Presser Feet

Use an open-toe appliqué foot. It allows you to see where you are stitching. In addition, it allows the appliqué piece to rest against the inside edge of the foot as you are stitching.

Open-toe
appliqué foot

The edge-stitching foot is another good choice. It has a blade down the center. Place the blade on the background fabric next to the appliqué piece you are stitching.

Three Little Things

You can have the largest fabric stash or more threads than anyone else, but in the end, it is all about the sewing machine. Treat her well and she will treat you well in return.

Here is my "to do before I start" checklist:

- Remove all lint buildup under the throat plate and in the bobbin area.
- Insert a new needle.
- Oil the race in the bobbin.

Machine Stitches

The Invisible Appliqué Stitch

Check your owner's manual to see if your machine has an invisible appliqué stitch and become familiar with setting the stitch length and stitch width.

Use the needle up/needle down option if it's available on the machine.

The Blindhem Stitch

This stitch is perfect for giving a quilt an invisible hand appliquéd look. Start the stitch with a few straight stitches in the background right next to the appliqué. After several straight stitches, the needle makes one zigzag, biting the appliqué fabric, and then moving back to the background fabric. Repeat the series of stitches to complete the appliqué. You will hear the machine in your head going, "stitch, stitch, stitch, stitch, bite."

Let's Appliqué

The open-toe appliqué foot is shown in these photos. Contrasting pink thread is used so you can see the stitches.

When you put the thread on the thread holder, make sure it is unwinding from the back.

Always test the appliqué blind hemstitch on a practice piece first.

Start with the stitch length and width both set to 1. The needle will move to the right needle position.

Fold a piece of fabric back on itself so you can place the appliqué foot in the groove. Guide the fabric so that the straight stitches are on the right side of that groove.

When you feel comfortable stitching with length 1 and width 1, try going to a smaller length and width.

Position the appliqué under the needle. Use the hand wheel to put the needle in the background fabric right next to the edge of the appliqué. Draw the bobbin thread to the top and lay the threads under the appliqué foot and to the back.

Take a stitch or two forward and then a stitch backwards to lock the stitches.

Use your left hand to gently guide the appliqué. Take a few stitches until you see the needle zigzag to the other side and "bite" the fabric. That was easy!

When coming to a point, stitch down to the end of the point.

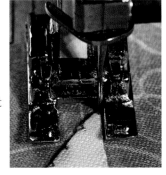

With the needle down, pivot the fabric and continue to sew.

When sewing a curve, take your time. Make sure to keep the inside edge of the appliqué foot tucked right against the appliqué piece you are sewing.

With the needle in the down position, lift the presser foot, and pivot as many times as is necessary. Take your time. It will become second nature to you.

Stitch a couple of stitches past where you started. Backstitch once. Snip the threads. You are finished! Practice makes perfect. It really does.

Here, you can see the difference between using cotton thread and monofilament thread.

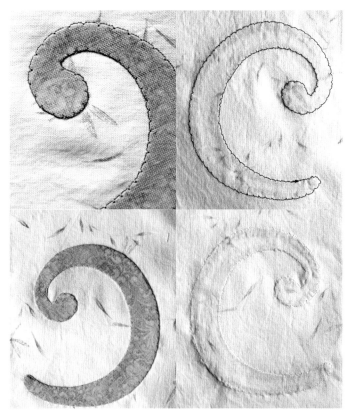

Projects

Appliqué

Poppies

27" x 32"

Size of appliquéd center panel: 19" x 25"

Designed, machine appliquéd, and machine quilted by Linda M. Poole

Fabric Requirements

Background: 20½" x 22½" rectangle of a light color
20½" x 5" rectangle of brown

Leaves: 1 fat quarter each of light, medium, and dark green

Vase: 1 fat quarter of multicolored blue/green

Flowers: 1 fat quarter of graduated orange/red

Stems: 14" of green bias tape

Prepare the templates and the appliqué pieces according to the Glue Stick Appliqué Technique described on pages 11–13.

To prepare the background, sew the brown rectangle to the bottom of the light rectangle. Press the seam allowances toward the brown.

Use the POPPIES templates on pages 33–37.

Step :

1 Glue F1 to F2 to F3 to F4. Appliqué together.

2 Glue F to unit F1-F2-F3-F4. Appliqué together.

3 Glue G1 to G2 to G3 to G4 to G5 to G6 to G7. Appliqué together.

4 Glue G to unit G1-G2-G3-G4-G5-G6-G7. Appliqué together.

5 Glue flower unit F to flower unit G. Appliqué together.

6 Glue H1 to H2 to H3 to H4 to H5 to H6 to H7 to H8 to H9. Appliqué together.

Glue H to unit H1-H2-H3-H4-H5-H6-H7-H8-H9. Appliqué together.

Glue flower unit H to flower unit F-G. Appliqué together.

7 Repeat the glue/appliqué process for flowers A, B, C, D, and E.

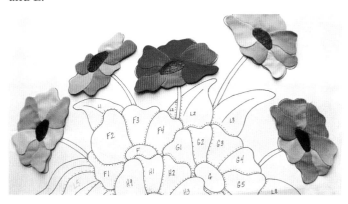

8 Glue L2 to L3. Appliqué together.

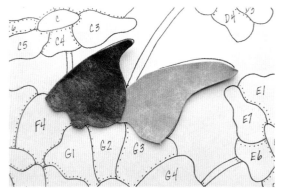

9 Glue or iron the bias tape stem to piece L2 leaving a ¼" seam allowance to go under flower units C and F. Appliqué both sides of the stem to leaf L2.

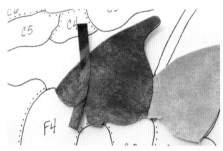

10 Repeat the glue/ appliqué process for leaf unit L4-L5-L6 and unit L8-L9.

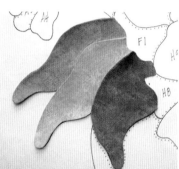

11 Glue the F-G-H flower unit, the leaf units, and the individual leaf pieces together. Appliqué together.

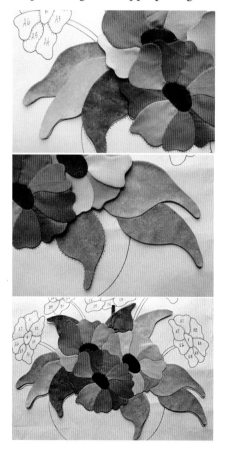

12 Glue V to V1 to V2 to V3 to V4. Appliqué together.

13 Glue the vase unit to the F-G-H flower/leaf unit. Appliqué together.

14 Glue or iron the bias tape stems on the traced lines on the background fabric, leaving a ¼" seam allowance on each. Appliqué both sides of the stems. Glue each flower unit and place it over the seam allowance of each stem.

15 Glue the vase and flower appliqué unit to the background. Appliqué.

Finishing

Step:

1 Trim the background fabric from behind the appliqués and remove the freezer paper or fusible water-soluble stabilizer as directed on page 13.

2 Trim the background to 19½" x 25½". Add borders as desired.

Painted Appliqué

Poppies

22½" x 25½"

Size of appliquéd center panel: 22" x 25"

Designed, machine appliquéd, and machine quilted by Linda M. Poole

Fabric Requirements

Background: 23½" x 23½" rectangle of a light color
        23½" x 5" rectangle of brown

Leaves: 1 fat quarter each of light, medium, and dark green

Vase and Flowers: ½ yard PFD or white, tightly woven 100% cotton

Stems: 14" of green bias tape

Art Supplies

InkFusion Fabric Medium

Derwent Inktense Water-Soluble Ink Pencils:
    Poppy Red, Sun Yellow, Tangerine, Sherbet Yellow, and Chili Red

Tulip Soft Fabric Paint:
    Grape Matte, White, and Periwinkle Matte

Prepare the PFD and templates for the poppies and vase according to the Painted Appliqué Technique 2 on pages 15–16.

Prepare the leaf templates and appliqué pieces according to the Glue Stick Appliqué Technique on pages 11–13.

Use the POPPIES template on pages 33–37.

Step :

1 Outline the edges of each flower petal of flower F with Tangerine and firmly color random sections. Color the remaining areas with Sun Yellow blending into the Tangerine. Color the middle inside edges with Poppy Red blending into the other colors.

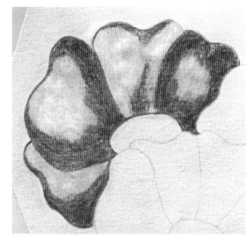

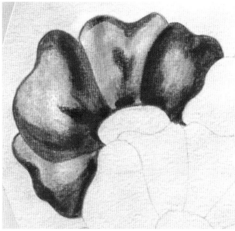

2 Dip a small paintbrush into InkFusion, putting just a tad on the brush, and paint each petal.

Tip : Here's what a "tad" looks like.

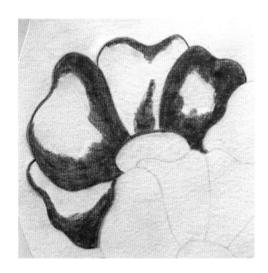

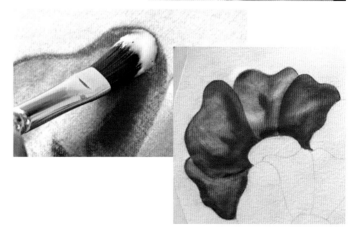

3 Repeat the above steps for the G flower, making each colored area a little different from the last.

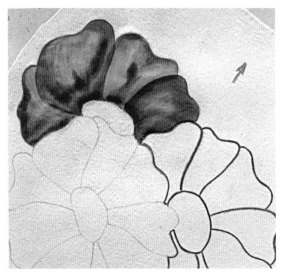

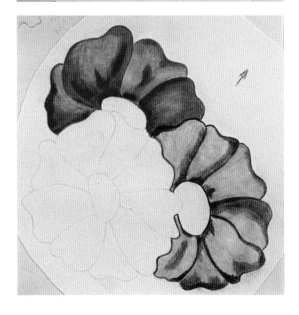

4 Dip a small paintbrush into InkFusion, putting just a tad onto the brush, and paint each petal.

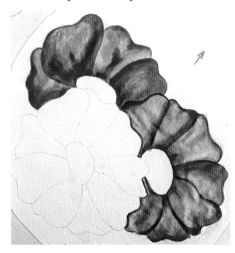

5 Continue coloring the H flower. When a petal of one flower touches another flower petal, make sure you do not have the same colors next to one another in order to distinguish the two different flowers.

6 Pressing firmly, color the bottom centers of each flower with Willow.

7 Lightly color the flower centers with Willow and Mustard. Be sure to blend the Mustard into the Willow. Dip a small paintbrush into InkFusion, putting just a tad onto the brush, and paint the centers.

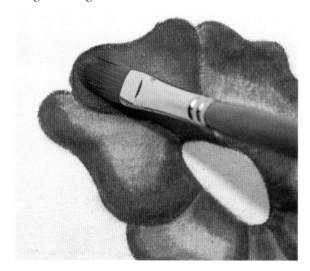

8 When coloring the remaining flowers, change the placement of colors.

9 Experiment with painting InkFusion over a darker color blending into a lighter color and vice versa.

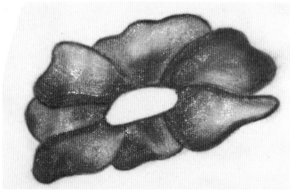

10 Finish painting the remaining flowers.

11 Pour a small amount of Grape Matte, White, and Periwinkle Matte into separate small containers or on an artist palette.

12 Start by outlining the top edge of the vase with Grape. Then, finish coloring the rest of the vase with Grape.

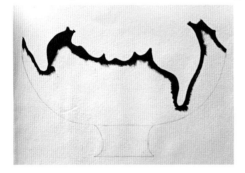

13 In a separate container, mix Grape and Periwinkle with just a spot of White. To add shading, paint the center of the main body with this new color.

14 If the highlight color from above is too light, add a little more Grape to the mixture and paint sparingly into the highlight color. Blend.

15 Dip the edge of the brush into Grape and paint a fine line between V and V1. Paint V1 using the same process and outline the bottom edge with Grape.

16 Paint the tops of V2 and V3 with Periwinkle. Paint a small mixture of Grape and White on both ends blending into the Periwinkle. Paint V4 with Grape.

17 Refer to the Poppies appliqué pattern on pages 33–37 to piece the background and appliqué all of the pieces and bias tape to the background.

Finishing

Step :

1 Trim the background fabric from behind the appliqués and remove the freezer paper or fusible water-soluble stabilizer as directed on page 13.

2 Trim the background to 22½" x 25½". Add borders as desired.

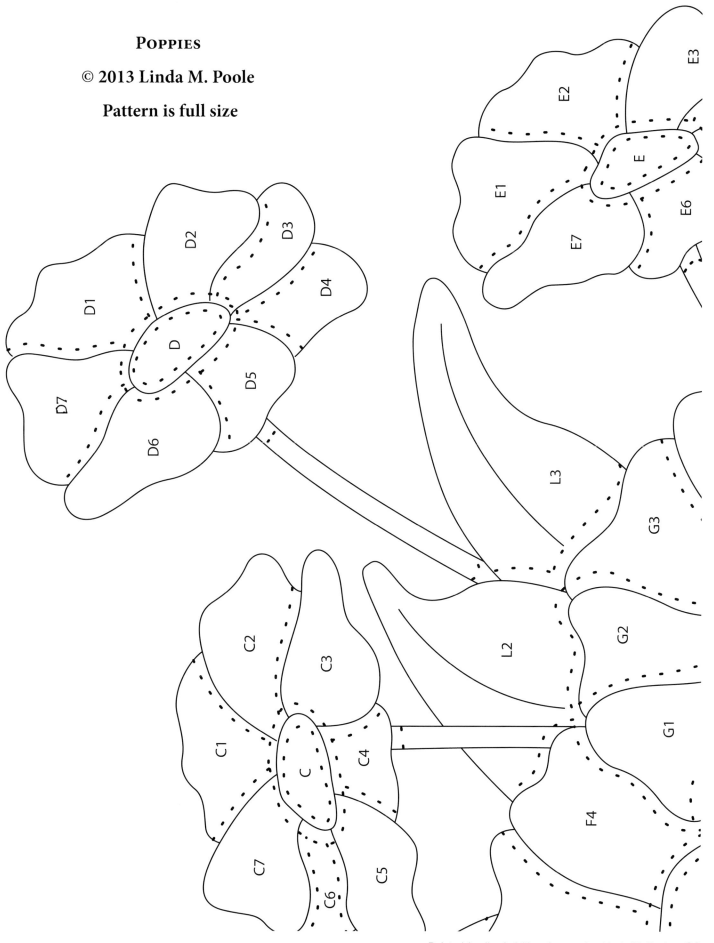

Poppies

© 2013 Linda M. Poole

Pattern is full size

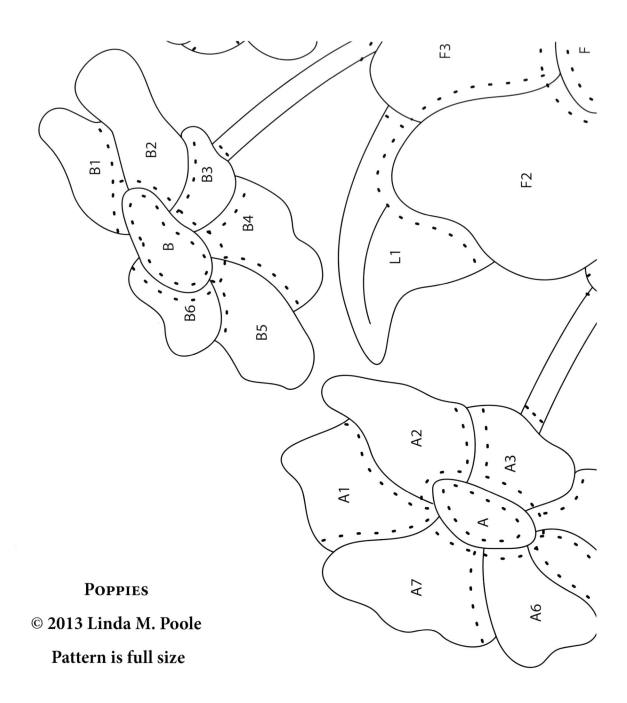

Poppies

© 2013 Linda M. Poole

Pattern is full size

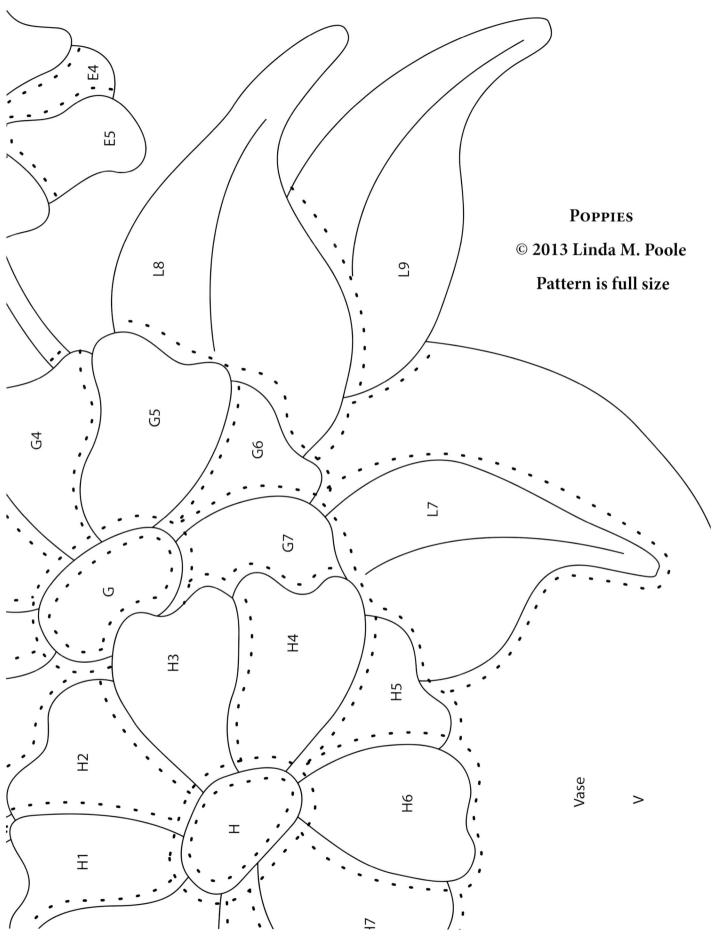

POPPIES

© 2013 Linda M. Poole

Pattern is full size

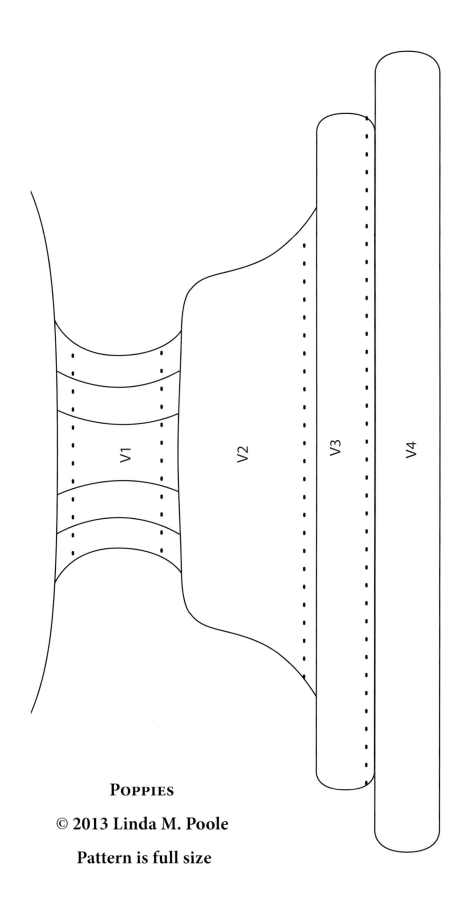

V1

V2

V3

V4

Poppies

© 2013 Linda M. Poole

Pattern is full size

Appliqué

Hello Sunshine

29" x 22"

Size of appliquéd center panel: 25" x 18"

Designed, machine appliquéd, and machine quilted by Linda M. Poole

Fabric Requirements

Background: 26½" x 19½" rectangle of a light color

Leaves: 1 fat quarter each of light, medium, and dark green

Bird: Large scraps

Tree Branches: Large scraps of various browns

Eye: Scrap of black

Prepare the templates and the appliqué pieces according to the Glue Stick Appliqué Technique described on pages 11–13.

Use the HELLO SUNSHINE template on pages 40–41.

For this project, disregard the red lines on the template.

Step :

1 Glue 11 to 12. Appliqué together.

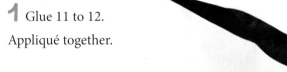

2 Glue 14 to 15. Appliqué together.

3 Glue piece 16 and 16a to unit 14-15. Appliqué together.

4 Glue L to 13 to R to 13a. Appliqué together.

5 Glue unit 11-12 to unit L-13-R-13a. Appliqué together.

6 Glue unit 11-12-L-13-R-13a to unit 14-15-16-16a. Appliqué together. Glue and appliqué the branch to the background.

Top Tree Branch

7 Glue A to B to C. Appliqué together. Glue and appliqué the branch to the background.

Bird

8 Glue 2 to 3. Glue 5 to 6. Glue 8 to 7a to 9. Appliqué the glued areas.

9 Glue unit 5-6 to 4 Appliqué together. Glue unit 8-7a-9 to 7. Appliqué together. Glue unit 4-5-6 to unit 7-8-7a-9. Appliqué together.

10 Glue unit 4-5-6-7-8-7a-9 to unit 2-3. Appliqué together.

11 Add the tail (10), beak (1), and eye. Appliqué together.

12 Glue and appliqué the bird to the background.

The Sun

13 Slip the large sunrays under the circular piece. Then, slip the smaller sunrays underneath. Appliqué together.

14 Glue and appliqué the sun to the background.

The Leaves

15 Use the master pattern for placement. Glue and appliqué the leaves to the background. Add more leaves if you want a fuller tree.

Finishing

Step :

1 Trim the background fabric from behind the appliqués and remove the freezer paper or fusible water-soluble stabilizer as on page 13.

2 Trim the background to 25½" x 18½". Add borders as desired.

Hello Sunshine

© 2013 Linda M. Poole

Pattern is full size

Hello Sunshine

© 2013 Linda M. Poole

Pattern is full size

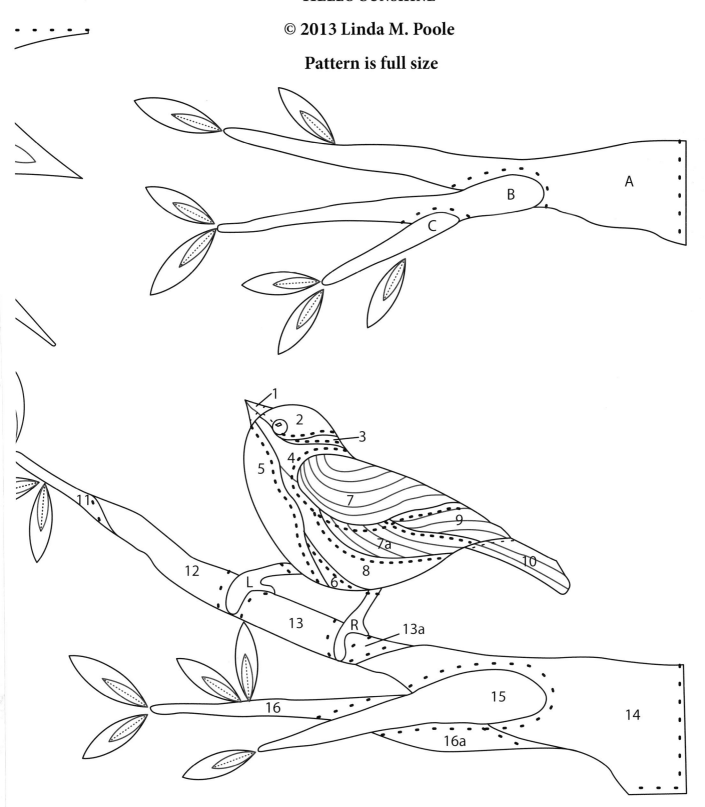

Painted Appliqué

Hello Sunshine

32" x 25½"

Size of appliquéd center panel: 25½" x 19"

Designed, painted, machine appliquéd, and machine quilted by Linda M. Poole

Fabric Requirements

Background: 27" x 20½" of a light blue

Tree: Assortment of browns, fat eighth of each

Legs: Scrap of gray

Bird, Leaves, and Sun: ½ yard PFD or white, tightly woven 100% cotton

Art Supplies

InkFusion Fabric Medium

Derwent Inktense Water-Soluble Ink Pencils:
Sun Yellow, Tangerine, Chili Red, Fuchsia, Sea Blue Iris Blue, Teal Green, Black, Apple Green, Violet, and Poppy Red

Black fabric marker and other markers, as desired

Prepare the PFD or white cotton fabric and the templates for the bird, leaves, and sun according to the Painted Appliqué Technique 1 as described on page 14.

Use the Hello Sunshine template on pages 40–41.

Prepare the templates and appliqués for the legs and tree branches according to the Glue Stick Appliqué Technique on pages 11–13.

Step :

1 Pressing firmly, color the inside shape in the leaves with Apple Green. Pressing firmly, color the outside of that shape in the leaves with Teal Green.

Dip a small paintbrush into InkFusion fabric medium, putting just a tad on the brush and paint each area of the leaf separately. When dry, add a touch of Teal Green around the inside shape and at the bottom of each leaf. Lightly paint over with InkFusion.

Tip :

Here's what a "tad" looks like.

When dry, outline the shapes with a black fabric marker and add tiny dots down the inside shape.

2 Pressing firmly, color the beak of the bird (1) with Sun Yellow. Lightly outline beak and accent the bottom corner with Tangerine. Dip a small paintbrush into InkFusion, putting just a tad onto the brush, and paint the beak.

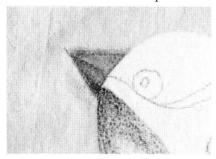

3 Pressing firmly, color the top and bottom corners of the belly (5) with Chili Red. Continue to lightly color the top and bottom edges of the belly. Using even pressure, color the center of the belly with Sun Yellow, blending into the outer edges of the Chili Red.

4 Lightly color over the Sun Yellow with Tangerine blending into the Chili Red.

5 Dip the paintbrush into InkFusion and paint the Chili Red at the bottom, blending down over the bottom edge. Paint the bottom red edge pulling the brush upward. Paint from the center, blending into the red sections.

6 Using even pressure, firmly color (8) with Fuchsia, leaving the center open for another color.

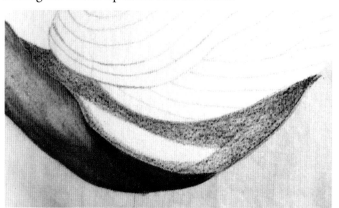

7 Using even pressure, color the open area with Orange.

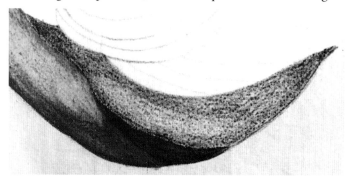

8 Dip the paintbrush into InkFusion and paint (8) from the center, blending into the fuchsia.

Using even pressure, color (6) with Chili Red, then paint it with InkFusion.

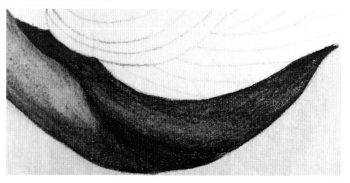

9 Using even pressure, outline the lines within (7a) with Sea Blue. Color within each line leaving open slivers in the center of each row.

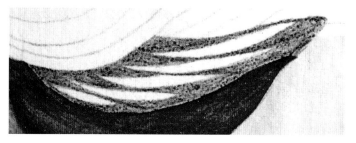

10 Using even pressure, color the open slivers with Iris Blue.

11 Dip the paintbrush into InkFusion and paint, blending from the center to the outer color.

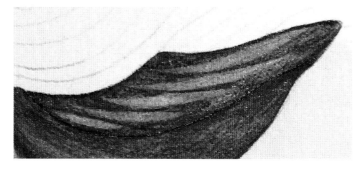

12 Outline section (7) and all the lines within it with Teal Green.

13 Using even pressure, color inside the lines using Teal Green, leaving open slivers in the center of each row. Lightly color the open slivers with Teal Green. Dip the paintbrush into InkFusion and paint each sliver, blending from the center out.

14 Using firm pressure, color the edges and corners of (3) with Fuchsia. Lightly color the rest of (3) with the same color. Dip the paintbrush into InkFusion and paint from the center blending into the outer color.

Using even pressure, color the top of (2) with Teal Green. Color the center and bottom with Apple Green.

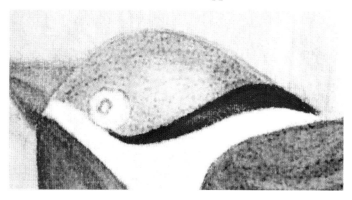

15 Dip the paintbrush into InkFusion and paint from the center, blending into the outer corners.

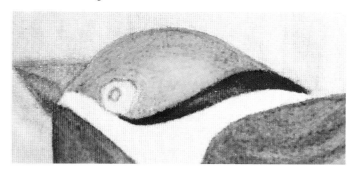

16 Using even pressure, outline the eye with Iris Blue, adding firm pressure at the top. Leave a little white square open without any color. Dip a paintbrush into InkFusion and paint the eye around the open square.

Using firm pressure, color the edges and corners of the top portion of (4) with Black. Lightly color the rest with the same color. Dip a paintbrush into InkFusion and paint the black.

17 Using even pressure, outline the lines within (9) with Violet. Color within each line, leaving open slivers in the center of each row.

Using even pressure, color the open slivers with Fuchsia. Dip a paintbrush into InkFusion and paint (9). Let the painted bird dry.

18 Using a window or light box, outline the eye, centerline in beak, and traced lines with a fabric marker. Have fun and draw shapes in the wing.

19 Complete the bird appliqué as directed in the painted appliqué section on page 14.

20 Evenly color an arc on the sun as shown with Sun Yellow. Press firmer when coloring the outside edge.

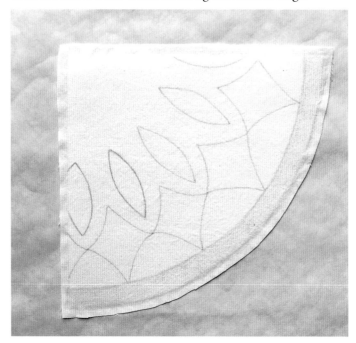

21 Lightly color over the Sun Yellow with Tangerine. Color in the middle of the shape with Poppy Red.

22 Dip a paintbrush into InkFusion and paint one color at a time. Drag the brush to make a shape as shown in the photo.

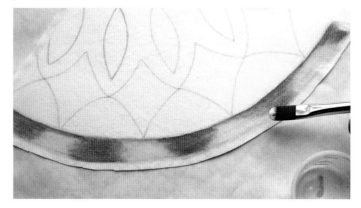

23 Color the outside edges of each shape with Violet pressing harder on the top and bottom. Color the center with Tangerine.

24 Dip a paintbrush into InkFusion and paint one side of the shape and then the other side. Let the two colors blend in the center.

25 Color the tops and edges of each diamond shape with Sun Yellow. Color the center with Fuchsia. Dip a paintbrush into InkFusion and paint the Sun Yellow, blending into the Fuchsia.

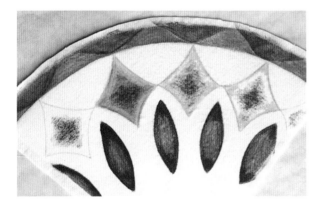

26 Using the photo as inspiration, have fun making shapes. Be sure to blend the colors into one another before painting with InkFusion.

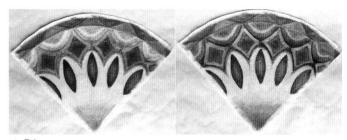

27 Continue coloring and painting the rays of the sun. Trim and glue the edges of the appliqués as directed in the painted appliqué section on page 14. Slip the large sunrays under the circular piece and then slip smaller sunrays underneath.

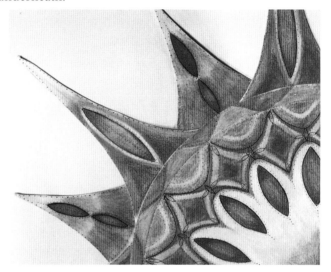

Anything you draw, color, and paint will be beautiful. Experiment and have fun!

28 Add dots and outlining features to the design. Use an Identi-pen, Prismacolor Marker, Gelly Roll pens, or fabric marker of your choice to bring the design to life. These pens come in a variety of colors.

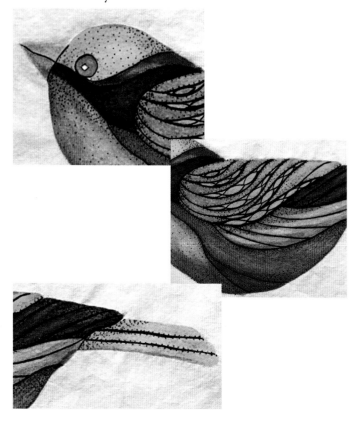

Test making dots on a blank piece of fabric. Try your hand at making tiny dots and some larger dots. You can shade areas by making a cluster of little dots that migrate outwards and get lighter and further apart from one another. A good example is underneath the wing in the blue area in the photo above.

If dots are not your cup of tea, a design looks just as beautiful without them.

Try outlining different areas and adding little doodles.

You can color, paint, outline, and add dots for even more touches after the quilting is finished.

Refer to the HELLO SUNSHINE Appliqué project on pages 38–40 and replace the appliquéd bird and sun with the painted pieces.

Finishing

Step :

1 Trim the background fabric from behind the appliqués and remove the freezer paper or fusible water-soluble stabilizer as directed on page 13.

2 Trim the background to 26" x 19½". Add borders as desired.

Appliqué

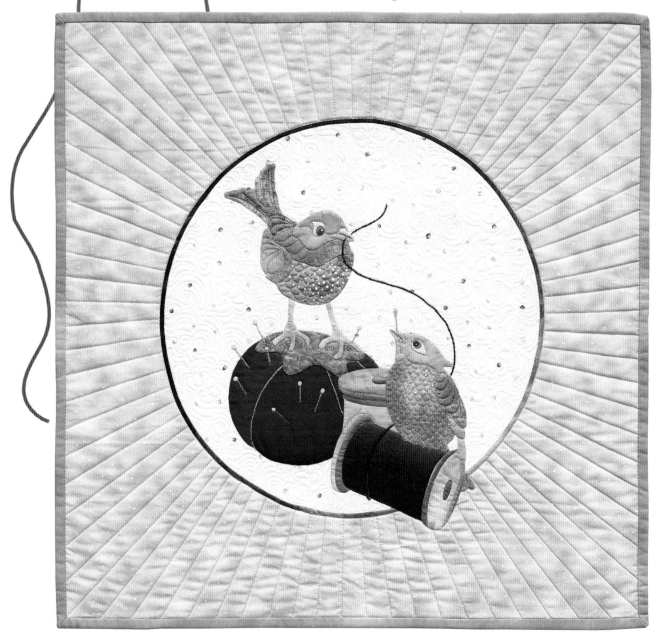

Little Helpers

24½" x 24½"

Size of appliquéd center panel: 16" x 16"

Designed and machine appliquéd by Linda M. Poole.
Machine quilted by Pamela Joy Dransfeldt, Camarillo, California.

Fabric Requirements

Background: 25½" x 25½" square of a light blue

Circle: 17½" x 17½" square of a light color

Birds, Spools, and Pincushion: large scraps

Supplies

Lightweight interfacing: 20" x 20"

Bias Tape: 48" of ¼" bias tape for around the circle

Embroidery floss

Yellow fabric paint

Prepare the templates and the appliqué pieces according to the Glue Stick Appliqué Technique described on pages 11–13.

Tip : If the fabric has enough shading in it, eliminate making pieces 21 and 22 separately and make as one piece.

Step :

1 After making templates 24 and 33 and before ironing fabric to them, cut a slit on one side of each template. Cut out the center oval.

2 Paper clip pieces together for better organization. For instance, clip all of the pieces for one bird together; clip all of the pieces for the second bird together; etc. When it is time to assemble the appliqués, all the parts will be in hand.

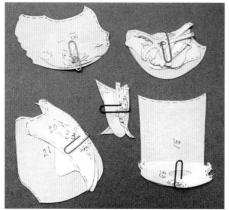

3 Glue 25 to 24 to 26 to 27 to 28. Appliqué together.

4 Glue 29 to 30 to 31 to 32 to 33 to 34. Appliqué together.

5 Glue 23 to 19 to 22 to 21 to 20. Appliqué together.

6 Lay out the prepared appliqué pieces for the two birds. It is easier to organize them.

7 Glue 5 to 7 to 6. Appliqué together. Glue 9 to 10. Appliqué together. Glue 1 to 2 to 3 to 4. Appliqué together. Glue unit 9-10 to unit 1-2-3-4. Appliqué together.

8 Glue 8 to unit 5-6-7. Appliqué together.

9 Glue unit 5-6-7-8 to unit 1-2-3-4-9-10. Appliqué together.

10 With a blue fabric marker, color a circle for the eye. With a black fabric marker, color a black oval at the front of the eye. Dab a dot of white paint in the black oval as shown in the photo. Glue the eye to the appropriate area and appliqué.

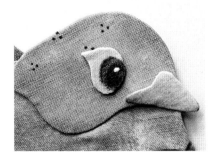

11 Glue the bird's legs (R and L) under the appliquéd body. Appliqué together. Glue the bird's feet to the bird (19). Appliqué together.

12 Glue 14 to 15 to 16. Glue 11 to 12 to 13. Appliqué the glued areas. Color, glue, and appliqué the eye as directed for the first bird.

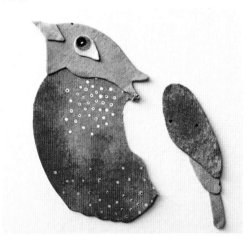

13 Glue unit 11-12-13 to unit 14-15-16. Glue the optional feet (R2 and L2) to the bird. Appliqué together.

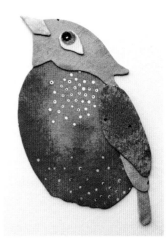

14 Glue the small spool to the large spool. Glue 17 and 18 to the large spool. Appliqué together.

15 Glue the bottom bird unit to the spools. Appliqué together.

16 Glue the bird/pincushion unit to the bird/spools unit. Appliqué together.

17 Make a circle from the square of light-colored fabric that measures 15½" in diameter for the background of Little Helpers. See pages 17–18 for instructions.

18 Place the circle over the master pattern. Glue the finished appliqué piece to the circle. Appliqué in place, beginning and ending ½" from where the circle meets the appliqué.

19 Place the appliqué over the master pattern. Lightly trace the thread and needle with a pencil.

20 Choose an embroidery floss to match the color of the large spool of thread. Use a large eye needle or embroidery needle and stem stitch along the traced line for the thread.

Use gray or metallic silver embroidery floss for the needle and pins. Use the end of a toothpick and dot yellow fabric paint to make the dots for the heads of the pins or use yellow floss and make French knots. Stem stitch the separations in the pincushion with green floss.

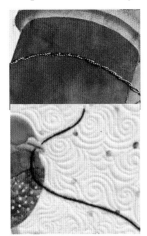

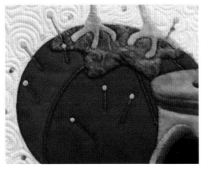

21 Lift up the edges of the appliqué where you did not stitch. Center the bias tape on the edge of the circle. Glue or iron the tape in place around the circle and appliqué, tucking a ¼" seam allowance of tape under the appliqué. Finish appliquéing the edges and sew the bias tape down.

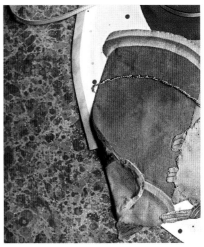

22 Turn the finished appliqué wrong-side up. Carefully make a slit inside the circle where you can see the appliqué stitches. Cut out the background fabric ¼" within the sewn appliqué stitches to lessen the bulk of fabric.

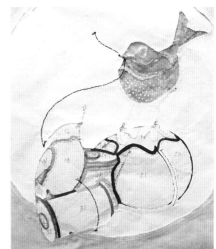

Finishing

Step:

1 Trim the background fabric from behind the appliqués and remove the freezer paper or fusible water-soluble stabilizer as directed on page 13.

2 Trim the background to 24¼" x 24¼". Add borders as desired.

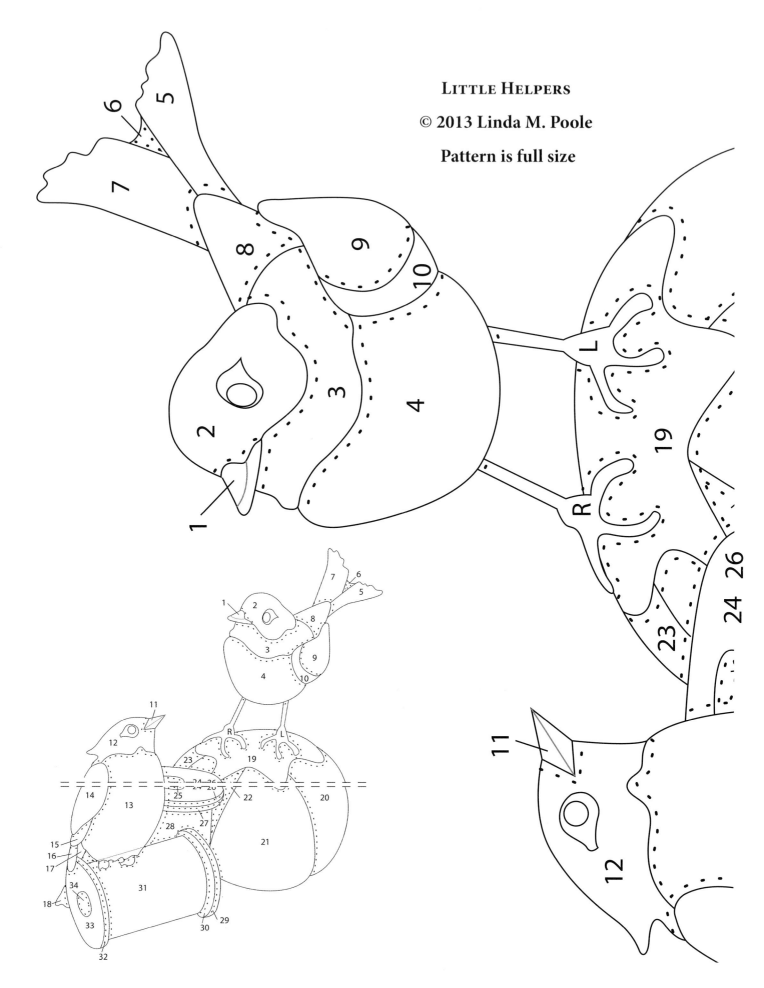

LITTLE HELPERS

© 2013 Linda M. Poole

Pattern is full size

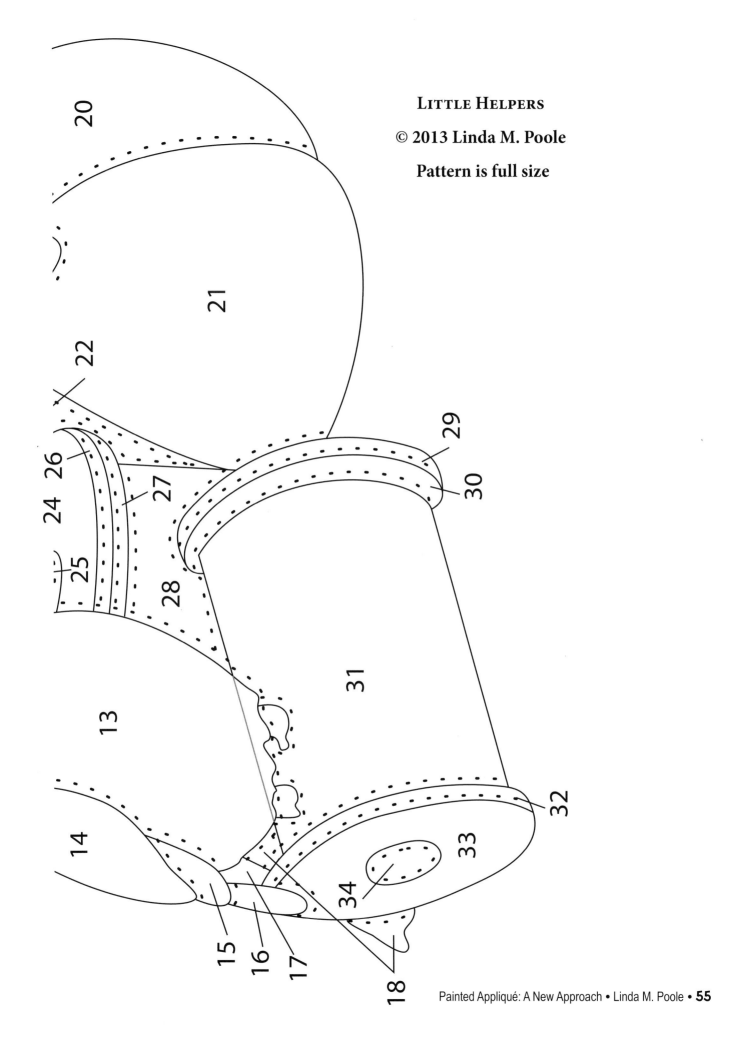

LITTLE HELPERS

© 2013 Linda M. Poole

Pattern is full size

Painted Appliqué

Little Helpers

21" x 26½"

Size of appliquéd center panel: 13½" x 18"

Designed, painted, and machine appliquéd by Linda M. Poole. Machine quilted by Pamela Joy Dransfeldt, Camarillo, California.

Fabric Requirements

Background: 22½" x 28" rectangle of blue

Oval: 15" x 19" rectangle of a light color

Appliqués: ¼ yard PFD or white, tightly woven 100% cotton

Supplies

Lightweight fusible interfacing: 16" x 20" rectangle

Bias Tape: 1½ yards

Art Supplies

Liquitex Soft Body Paints:
Iridescent Rich Gold, Burnt Sienna, Chromium, Oxide Green, Green Deep, Pyrrole Red, Pyrrole, Crimson, Dioxazine Purple, Cerulean Blue, Turner's Yellow, Titanium White, and Mars Black
Gelly Roll Pens: Metallic Dark Brown, Gold, and Red
Black fabric marker

Prepare the PFD or white cotton fabric and templates according to the Painted Appliqué Technique 1 as described on page 14.

Use the LITTLE HELPERS template on pages 54–55.

Step :

1 Trace the pincushion, birds, and spools of thread as separate pieces.

Tip : Try ironing a piece of freezer paper to the wrong side of the ready-to-paint piece and then pin it to two layers

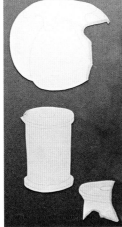

of cardboard or foam core to keep it stable while painting. When you are ready to paint the area where the pin is, move it to another area, pinning near the very edge of the place you are painting.

Put a good dollop of each color of paint on a coated paper plate, the shiny side of a piece of freezer paper, or a palette. Squirt one part InkFusion to two parts paint on each color and mix well.

2 Paint the legs (R and L) with Iridescent Rich Gold. Dip the paintbrush lightly in Burnt Sienna. With an almost dry brush, paint the right side of each leg and claw for shadowing.

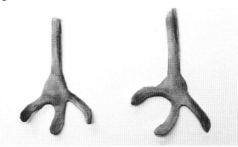

3 Paint piece 19 with Chromium Oxide Green. Paint the top with an almost dry brush loaded with Green Deep. Blend well.

4 Paint the pincushion with Pyrrole Red. Dip the brush into Pyrrole Crimson. With an almost dry brush, begin to shade by painting the outer edges of each wedge. Dry brush the areas within the pincushion to give it a worn look.

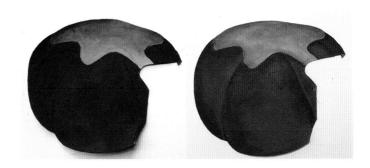

5 Paint the ends of each spool with Iridescent Rich Gold. Paint over the lines for the holes.

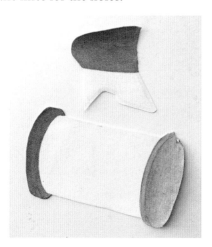

6 With an almost dry brush, paint with Burnt Sienna to shade the edges. Wipe the brush on a paper towel and drag the Burnt Sienna outward ever so slightly.

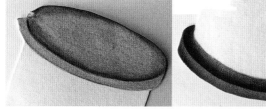

7 Paint the hole on both spools of thread with Burnt Sienna. Paint a small highlight as shown with Iridescent Rich Gold.

8 Mix Dioxazine Purple and Titanium White to lighten the purple to your liking. Paint the bottom portion of the spool on a diagonal with Dioxazine Purple. Paint on the diagonal and fill in with Dioxazine Purple as shown in the photo to give the illusion of shading.

9 Paint the belly of each bird with Iridescent Rich Gold.

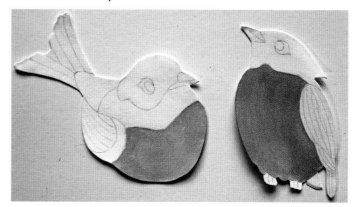

10 Paint the head of the bottom bird with Raw Sienna. Paint around the edges of the head and on top of and under the beak with just a tad of Burnt Sienna.

11 Paint the beak of the bottom bird with Turner's Yellow. Sparingly, shade with Raw Sienna. Use a marker to draw a line in the beak.

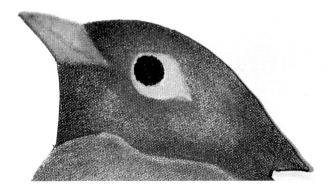

12 For the eye of the bottom bird, paint in and around the circle with Turner's Yellow. Paint the circle with Mar's Black. Make a small dot with Titanium White.

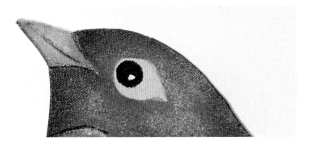

13 Paint both feet with Raw Sienna and highlight with Burnt Sienna.

14 With Raw Sienna, shade under the head, along the left side, and on the side next to the wing. Blend inward toward the center of the belly.

15 With brown and metallic gold Gelly Roll pens, make random dots on the belly. Draw a line separating the head from the belly with the brown pen. Draw the lines in the feet of the bottom bird.

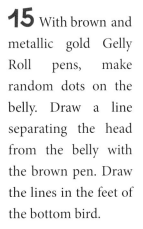

16 Paint the wings and tail with Raw Sienna. Lightly paint the feather lines with Burnt Sienna. Add highlights with Iridescent Rich Gold.

17 Paint the tail of the top bird with Raw Sienna. Add shading by painting Burnt Sienna and Iridescent Rich Gold here and there. Feel free to mix colors. The purpose is to separate the feathers with different colors.

Paint the back of the top bird with Iridescent Rich Gold. Highlight the area connecting to the tail and on the sides with just a tad of Raw Sienna on the brush.

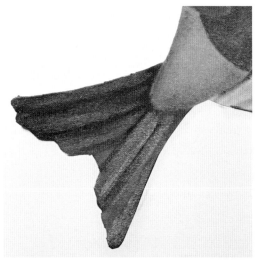

18 Use the brown Gelly Roll pen to add details. Make little dots going down each feather. Add random dots on the back with gold and red Gelly Roll pens.

19 Paint the head with Raw Sienna. Paint around the edges of the head and on top of and under the beak with just a tad of Burnt Sienna.

Paint the beak with Turner's Yellow. Sparingly, shade with Raw Sienna. Use a fabric marker to draw a line in the beak.

Paint the section under the head with Burnt Sienna. Highlight with Iridescent Rich Gold.

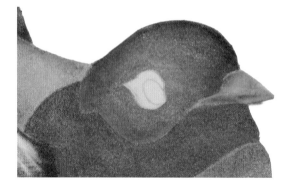

20 Paint in and around the eye with Turner's Yellow. Paint the circle with Mars Black. Make a small dot with Titanium White.

Add random brown dots in the section under the head with a brown Gelly Roll pen. Outline head, beak, and the section under head with the brown Gelly Roll pen.

21 Shade the right side and bottom of belly with Raw Sienna. Have a little fun making tiny and larger dots with different colors of Gelly Roll pens.

22 Paint the outside of the wing with Iridescent Rich Gold. Paint an arc next to the feathers with Raw Sienna. With Burnt Sienna, lightly paint inside the feathers near the rim of the wing and drag the paint strokes outward.

23 Shade the bottom and outside edges of the crescent area with Burnt Sienna. With a mixture of Raw Sienna and just a little Burnt Sienna, lightly paint over the feathers.

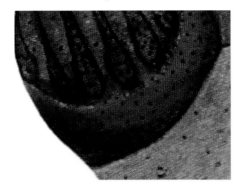

24 With a brown Gelly Roll pen, outline the feathers as shown. Add brown dots in the feathers and crescent shape.

25 Refer to the LITTLE HELPERS appliqué pattern on pages 54–55 for details on gluing and completing the appliqué.

26 Make an oval that is 13¼" x 17¼" when finished. See pages 18–19 for instructions. Replace the circle in the appliqué version with the oval.

Finishing

Step :

1 Trim the background fabric from behind the appliqués and remove the freezer paper or fusible water-soluble stabilizer as directed on page 13.

2 Trim the background to 21" x 26½". Add borders as desired.

Appliqué

Wings
45" x 45"

Designed and machine appliquéd by Linda M. Poole. Pieced and bound by Helen Umstead, Lords Valley, Pennsylvania.
Machine quilted by Sherry Rogers-Harrison, Normandy Park ,Washington.

Fabric Requirements

Background: 1¼ yards turquoise

Border: 1¼ yards turquoise, slightly lighter than the background

Stars, Half-Stars: 1 yard for pieces 1 and 3
                 1 yard for pieces 2 and 4

Star Flower: Large scraps

Butterfly Wings: Large scraps

Butterfly Body: 4" square of black

Dragonfly: Scraps in different values and colors

Honey Bee: Small scraps of yellow and off white

Hexagons: 12" square or fat quarter of yellow

Bird: Large scraps

Nest: Small fusible bias tape strips in a range of values, enough to cover the nest

Prepare all of the templates and the appliqué pieces according to the Glue Stick Appliqué Technique described on pages 11–13, except for the bias tape for the mama bird.

Star Appliqué

You will need to prepare templates and appliqué pieces for five stars. The star template is on page 64.

Step :

1 Fold the freezer paper or stabilizer sheet in half horizontally and in half vertically, making four layers. Place the folds on the vertical and horizontal centers of the master pattern. Trace one quadrant of the star appliqué template on page 64.

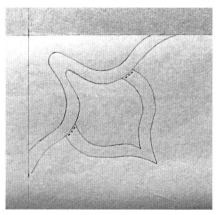

2 Staple inside of the traced lines to secure the layers. Cut through the four layers to make the templates.

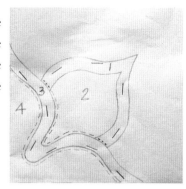

3 Iron piece 3 to your fabric and trim around the template leaving a ¼" seam allowance and turn under the inside edge of the shape, as well as the outside edge. Piece 4 will have none of the edges turned over and will be glued behind piece 3.

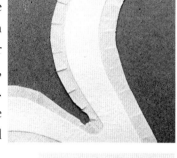

4 Glue 1 to 2 for all four quadrants. Appliqué together.

5 Glue 3 to 4. Appliqué together.

6 Glue the four 1-2 units to unit 3-4. Appliqué together.

Half-Star Appliqué

You will need to prepare templates and appliqué pieces for four Half-Stars using the template to the right.

To make the Half-Stars, trace half of the Star pattern onto freezer paper, adding a ¼" seam allowance beyond where the half ends.

Follow the Star assembly instructions on page 63.

Star Flower Appliqué

1

2

3

4

STAR
© 2013 Linda M. Poole
Pattern is full size
Place on fold

Place on fold

Use the Star Flower template on page 65.

1 Glue 1 to 2 for all five petals. Appliqué together.

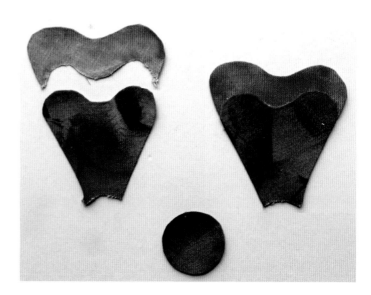

2 Glue the five 1-2 units to 3. Appliqué together.

3 Glue the Star Flower to a Star. Appliqué together.

Tip : For a different look, make the flower (except for piece 3) as one piece.

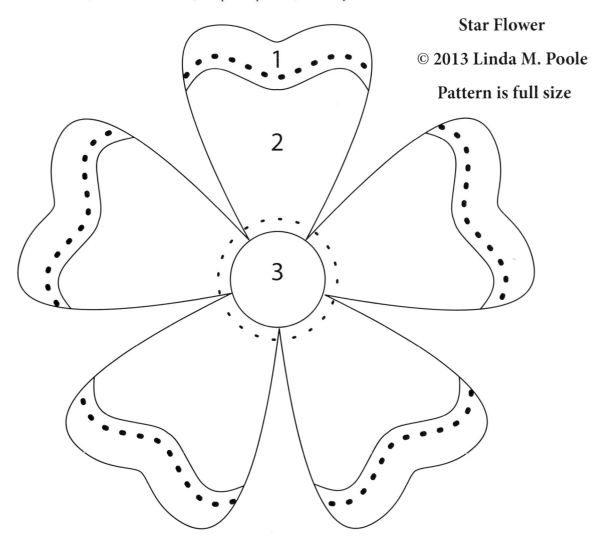

Star Flower

© 2013 Linda M. Poole

Pattern is full size

Butterfly Appliqué

Use the Butterfly template on page 67.

For this project, disregard the red lines on the template.

Step :

1 Glue 1L to 2L. Appliqué together. Glue 1R to 2R. Appliqué together.

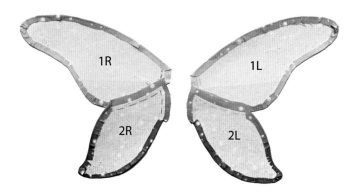

2 Glue units 1L-2L and 1R-2R to B. Appliqué together.

3 Glue the Butterfly to a Star. Appliqué together.

Butterfly

© 2013 Linda M. Poole

Pattern is full size

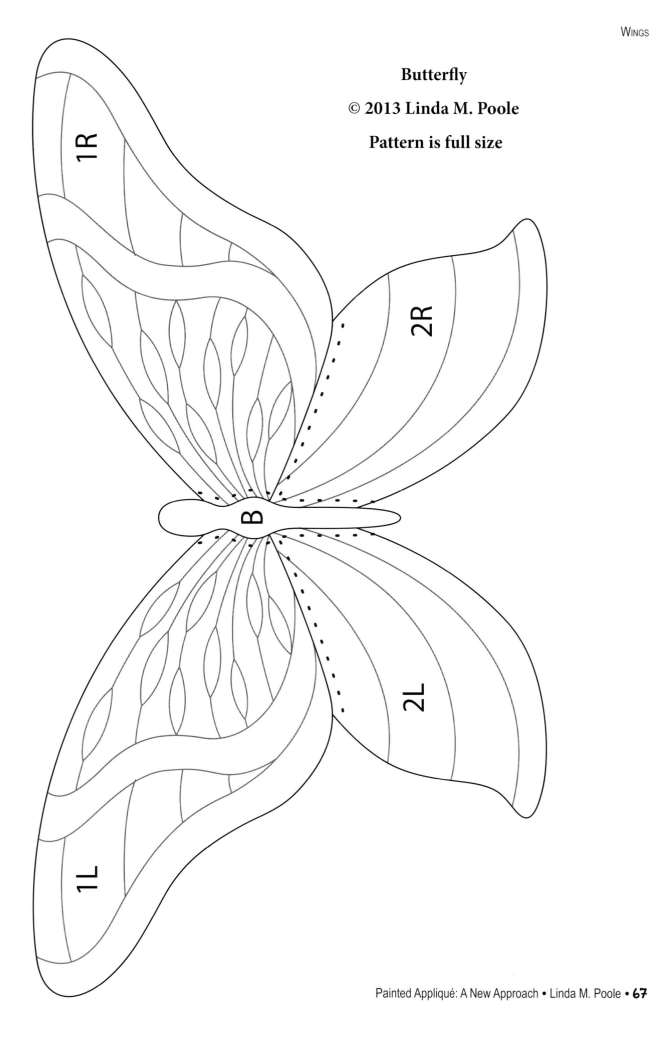

Dragonfly Appliqué

Use the Dragonfly template on page 69.

For this project, disregard the red lines on the template for the body.

Step :

1 Glue 1 to 2 to 3 to 4 to 5 to 6.

Appliqué together.

2 Glue 7L to 8L. Glue 7R to 8R. Appliqué the glued areas.

3 Glue units 7L-8L and 7R-8R to unit 1-2-3-4-5-6. Appliqué together.

4 Glue the Dragonfly to a Star. Appliqué together.

Dragonfly

© 2013 Linda M. Poole

Pattern is full size

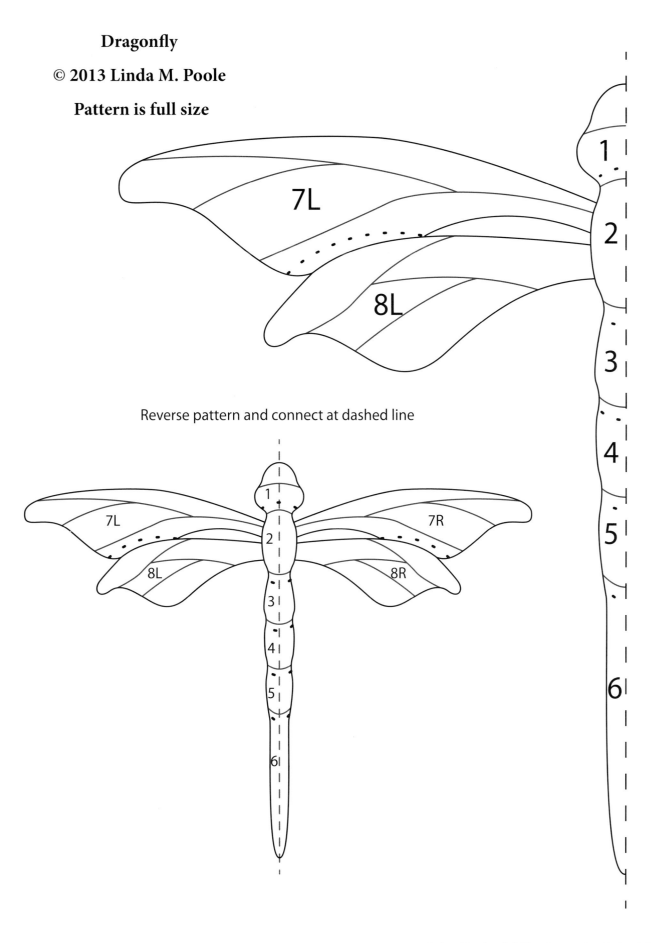

Reverse pattern and connect at dashed line

Honey Bee Appliqué

Use the Honey Bee template on page 71.

3 Glue 1 to 2 to 3. Appliqué together.

For this project, disregard the red lines on the template.

4 Glue both wings to unit 1-2-3. Appliqué together.

Step :

1 Using a black fabric marker, draw lines in the wings.

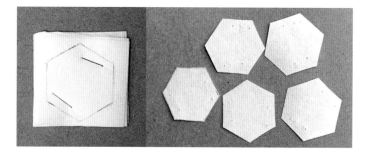

5 Trace one hexagon on freezer paper or a water-soluble stabilizer sheet. Layer four more sheets, all facing the same way with the shiny-side down, under the traced hexagon and staple together. Cut on the traced line and remove the staples.

2 Using a black fabric marker, color the top of the head (piece 1) and the stripes in the body (piece 3).

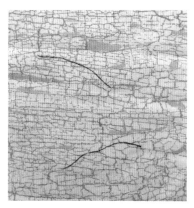

6 Glue the Honey Bee and the hexagons to the Star. Appliqué together.

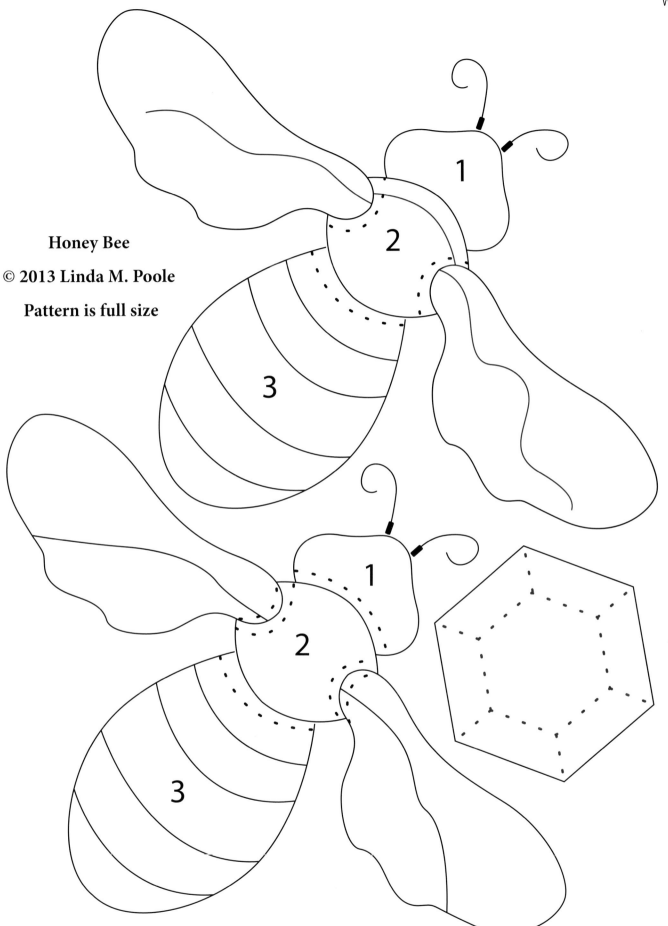

Honey Bee

© 2013 Linda M. Poole

Pattern is full size

Mama Bird Appliqué

Use the Mama Bird template on page 74–76.

For this project, disregard the red lines on the template.

Supplies

Teflon sheet

Black fabric marker

Scraps of fabric for bird

One beautiful spring day, I noticed a mama bird had made her nest on the top rail of our deck. I walked quietly into the house to get my camera and waited for her to return to her nest. Silently, I took pictures and studied her and the nest. The small twigs she gathered to make her new home looked like bias tape to me. Yes, nature can give us all kinds of ideas. That day, I began to sketch what I saw and to create this darling appliqué of the little bird and her nest.

Step:

1 Place the shiny side of a fusible water-soluble stabilizer sheet on top of the master pattern. Trace the outline of the nest. Cut the nest out on the traced line. Place the nest on a Teflon sheet before ironing the bias tape on top of it.

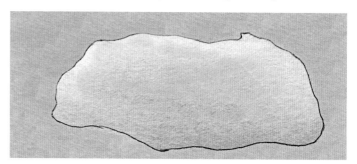

2 Using no steam, lightly iron down a few strips of fusible bias tape that overlap the edges. By lightly ironing them, you will be able to lift the fusible bias tape. Weave more bias tape strips over and under one another until the nest is filled. Press the bias tape firmly. Let the bias tape cool and lift the nest off the Teflon sheet. Machine stitch the bias tape to the stabilizer, making sure it is secure.

3 Glue 1 to 2 to 3. Appliqué together.

Glue the beak to the bird. Appliqué together.

Glue unit 1-2-3 to the bird. Appliqué together.

Color the bird's eye with a black marker.

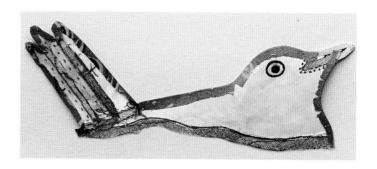

4 Glue the bird to the nest. Appliqué together.

5 Glue the bird/nest to the star appliqué. Appliqué together. Machine stitch the nest enough to hold it to the star.

Placing the Appliqués on the Wings Background

Step:

1 Cut a 36½" square from the background fabric.

2 Fold the background fabric in half vertically.

3 Lightly iron to make a crease. Fold it in half again vertically.

4 Lightly iron to make a crease. Open the fabric.

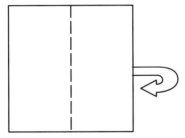

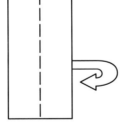

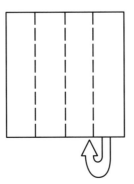

5 Now, fold the fabric in half horizontally. Lightly iron to make a crease. Fold in half again. Lightly iron to make a crease.

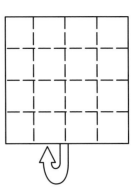

6 Open the fabric. There should be creases dividing the fabric into four equal sections vertically and horizontally. The intersecting creases are the center lines for the placement of the Star appliqué units.

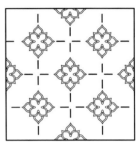

7 Glue the Half Stars at the center points of each side on the background. Appliqué.

8 Glue the Star Flower, Butterfly, Dragonfly, Honey Bee, and Mama Bird appliqués to the background, using the creases for alignment. Appliqué.

Finishing

Step:

1 Trim the background fabric from behind the appliqués and remove the freezer paper or fusible water-soluble stabilizer as directed in the Painted Appliqué Techniques chapter under Removing the Freezer Paper on page 13.

2 Add borders as desired.

Mama Bird

© 2013 Linda M. Poole

Pattern is full size

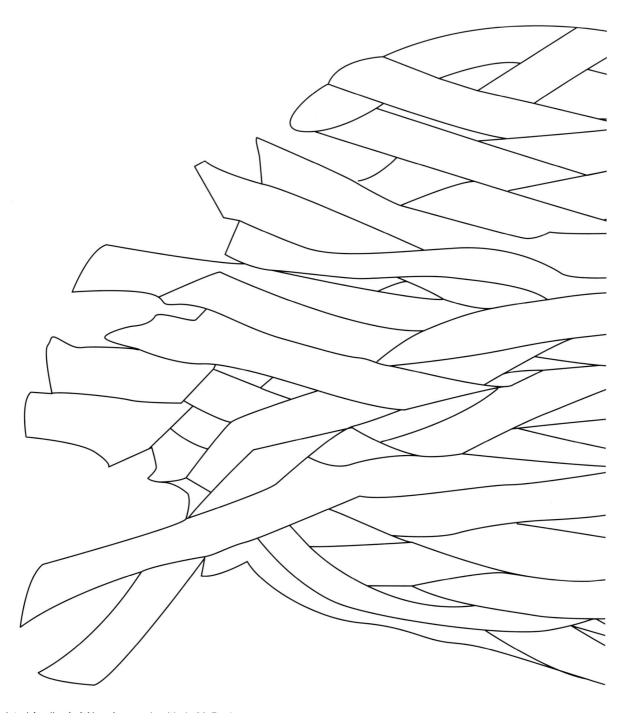

Mama Bird

© 2013 Linda M. Poole

Pattern is full size

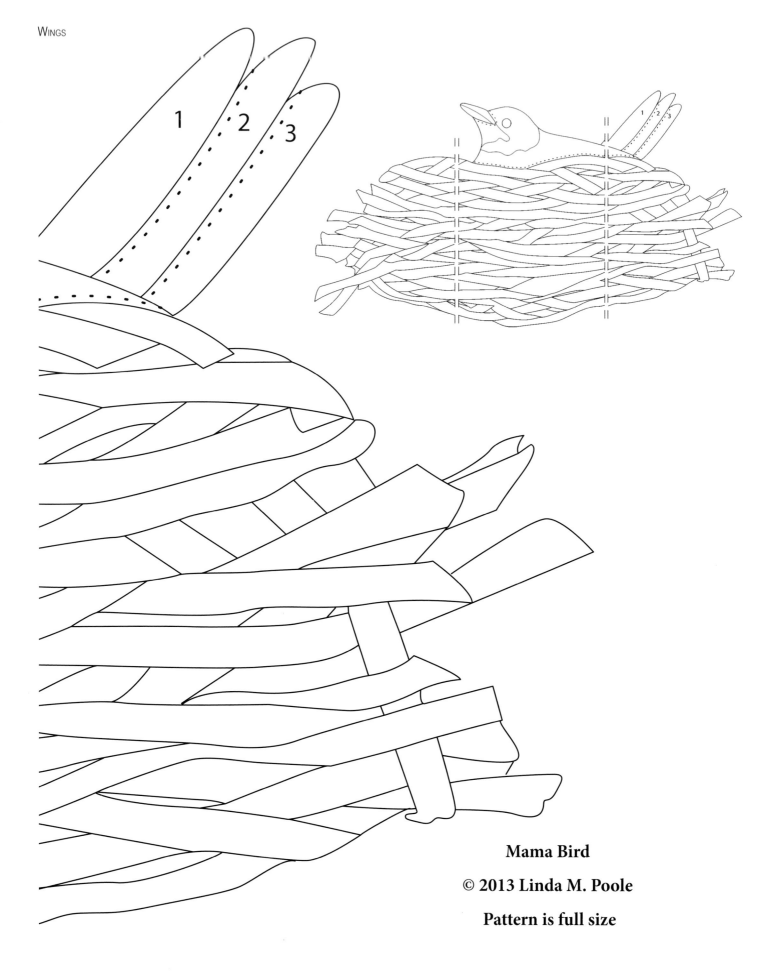

1

2

3

Mama Bird

© 2013 Linda M. Poole

Pattern is full size

Painted Appliqué

Star

Use the Star template on page 64. It is the background for the Butterfly Star Painted Appliqué, Dragonfly Star Painted Appliqué, Honey Bee Star Painted Appliqué, and Mama Bird Star Painted Appliqué.

The star is not a project by itself. Make one Star Painted Appliqué for each of the painted appliqué projects you choose.

Fabric Requirements

Appliqué: ½ yard PFD or white, tightly woven 100% cotton

Art Supplies

InkFusion Fabric Medium

Liquitex Soft Body Paints:
Titanium White, Cadmium Red, Yellow Medium, and Medium Magenta

Optional – Gelly roll or Sanford Colorific Gel markers

Use the Star Appliqué template and the Steps 1–6 construction information on pages 63–64.

Prepare the templates and the painted appliqué pieces according to the Painted Appliqué Technique 1 on page 14.

Step :

1 Fold the freezer paper or stabilizer in half horizontally. Fold in half vertically. Place the folds on the vertical and horizontal centers of the master pattern. Trace one quadrant.

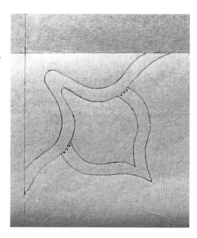

2 Staple inside of the traced lines to secure the layers. Cut through the four layers to make the template.

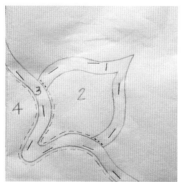

3 Refer to the photo to see where to add the scant ¼" seam allowances on pieces 3 and 4.

4 Mix together two parts Medium Magenta with one part Titanium White. Add more Titanium White, if desired. Paint all of the Pieces for 1 and 3 with the Medium Magenta/Titanium White mixture.

5 Paint the tips of each piece with a little Magenta and blend into the previous painted areas. Set aside to dry.

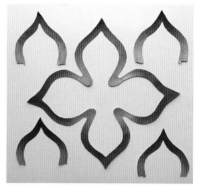

6 Mix together one part Yellow Medium and a drop or two of Cadmium Red Medium. Paint all four of the Piece 2s with Yellow Medium. Paint the bottom areas with the Yellow Medium/Cadmium Red Medium mixture.

7 Paint the Piece 4 with Yellow Medium. Paint outer areas with the Yellow Medium/Cadmium Red Medium mixture.

8 Glue and appliqué the pieces together as shown in the photos. Refer to the Star Appliqué pattern on page 64 for more details.

9 Paint the star lightly with InkFusion.

10 Use the Star Appliqué as directed in the pattern for your project.

More Options for Painting the Star

Use Gelly roll pens or Sanford Colorific Gel Markers to add dots on the edges of the Star pattern.

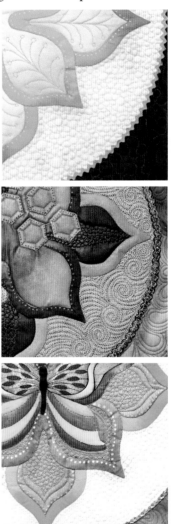

Painted Appliqué

Butterfly Star

20" x 20"

Size of appliquéd center panel: 16" x 16"

Designed, painted, and machine appliquéd by Linda M. Poole. Machine quilted by Lisa Sipes, Philadelphia, Pennsylvania.

Fabric Requirements

Background: 21½" x 21½" square of blue
17½" x 17½" square of a light color
Appliqué: ½ yard PFD or white, tightly woven
100% cotton

Art Supplies

Derwent Water-Soluble Ink Pencils:
Fuchsia, Sun Yellow, Apple Green, Field Green,
and Tangerine
Black fabric marker
InkFusion Fabric Medium

Use the Butterfly Appliqué template on page 67.

A star is the background for the Butterfly Star Painted Appliqué project. Instructions for the Star Painted Appliqué are on page 78.

You will need to prepare templates and appliqué pieces for one Butterfly.

Prepare the templates and the appliqué pieces according to the Painted Appliqué Technique 1 described on page 14.

Step :

1 Firmly outline and color all the pointed ovals with Fuchsia. Lightly color outside the lines.

2 Firmly color around the ovals with Sun Yellow. Color the rest of the section with Field Green.

3 Firmly color the vertical band with Sun Yellow. Firmly color the top and bottom with Tangerine.

Firmly color the next section with Apple Green. Firmly color with Field Green next to the yellow and tangerine band.

4 Firmly color the outer section with Fuchsia. Be sure to color harder in the top, bottom, and center areas.

5 Use colors in the following order, starting from the top: Apple Green, Tangerine, Sun Yellow, and Fuchsia. Color each section, pressing firmer at the inner edge of the wing, and outline the bottom edge of each section.

Color the body with the black marker.

Dip a small paintbrush into InkFusion, putting just a tad onto the brush, and paint the colored areas one at a time.

Clean the brush in water before going to a new color.

6 Use a black fine-tip fabric marker to draw all the traced lines in the upper wing sections. Make small dots on the outer edge and randomly sprinkle some within the design. Make dots on the traced lines in the lower wing sections.

Assemble the appliqué as directed in the Butterfly Appliqué project on page 66.

7 Glue the Butterfly to a Star Appliqué and appliqué together.

8 To make the circular background, refer to pages 17–18 or glue the appliqué to the background of your choice. Appliqué.

Finishing

Step :

1 Trim the background fabric from behind the appliqués and remove the freezer paper or fusible water-soluble stabilizer as directed on page 13.

2 Trim the background to 20½" x 20½". Add borders as desired.

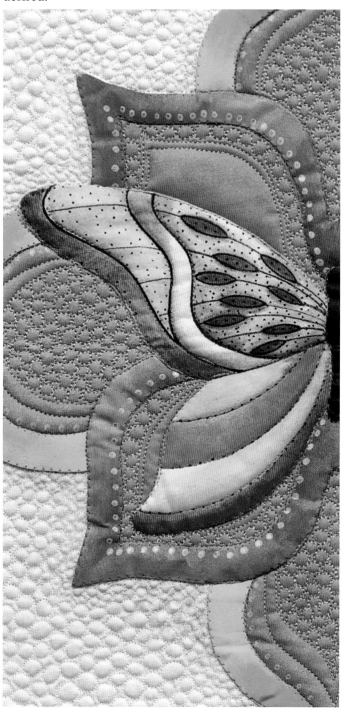

Painted Appliqué

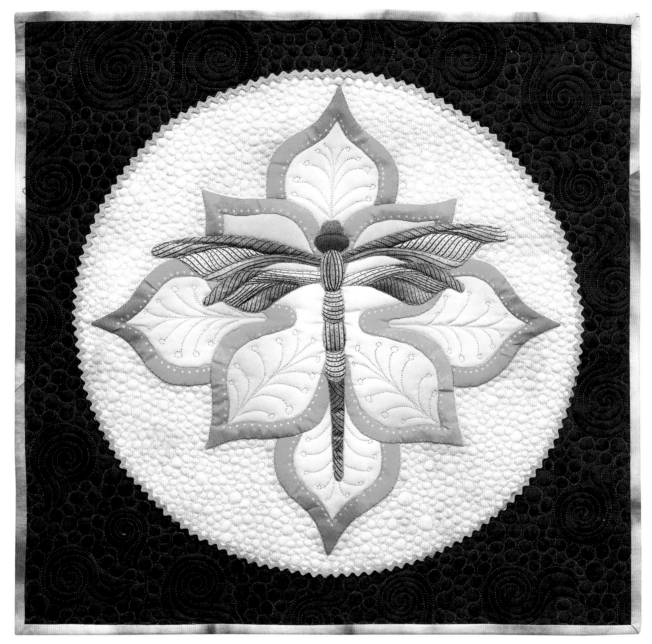

Dragonfly Star

20" x 20"

Size of appliquéd center panel: 16" x 16"

Designed, painted, and machine appliquéd by Linda M. Poole. Machine quilted by Lisa Sipes, Philadelphia, Pennsylvania.

Fabric Requirements

Background: 21½" x 21½" square of purple
17½" x 17½" square of a light color

Appliqué: ½ yard PFD or white, tightly woven 100% cotton

Art Supplies

PROfab Textile Paints:
Key Lime, Pearlescent, Magenta, Purple, and Caribbean Breeze

Black fabric marker

Use the Dragonfly Appliqué template on page 69.

A star is the background for the Dragonfly Star Painted Appliqué project. Instructions for the Star Painted Appliqué are on page 78. Prepare the templates and the appliqué pieces according to the Painted Appliqué Technique 1 described on page 14.

To make lighter paint colors, add PROfab Pearlescent Paint to each color.

Step :

1 Paint each section of 7L with a different color. Paint 7R as the mirror image.

2 Paint each section of 8L with a different color. Paint 8R as the mirror image.

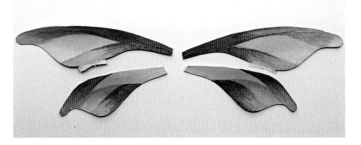

3 Draw squiggly lines within each section with the black marker. Each section should have the squiggly lines going a different direction from one another. Add dots.

Do this for all four wings. Again, 7R should be the mirror image of 7L, and 8R should be the mirror image of 8L.

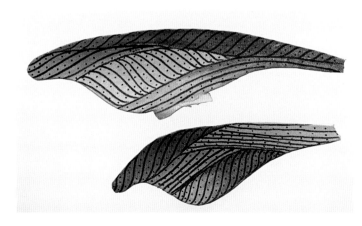

4 Paint the body as you did the wings. See the photo for suggestions.

5 Glue and complete the Dragonfly. See the Dragonfly Appliqué pattern on page 69 for more details.

Glue the Dragonfly to the Star Appliqué and appliqué together.

To make the circular background, refer to pages 17–18 or glue the appliqué to the background of your choice.

Finishing
Step :

1 Trim the background fabric from behind the appliqués and remove the freezer paper or fusible water-soluble stabilizer as directed on page 13.

2 Trim the background to 20½" x 20½". Add borders as desired.

Painted Appliqué

Honey Bee Star

20" x 20"

Size of appliquéd center panel: 16" x 16"

Designed, painted, and machine appliquéd by Linda M. Poole. Machine quilted by Lisa Sipes, Philadelphia, Pennsylvania.

Fabric Requirements

Background: 21½" x 21½" square of blue
             17½" x 17½" square of a light color

Appliqué: ½ yard PFD or white, tightly woven
     100% cotton

Art Supplies

PaintFusion Fabric Medium

Dry Pigment Paint by LuminArte:
     PE – 144 Dragonfly Wing and
     PE – 156 French Vanilla

Liquitex Soft Body Yellow Medium

Black fabric marker

Gelly Roll Pens

Sanford Colorific Gel Markers:
     Blue, Light Purple, Yellow, and Orange

Use the Honey Bee Appliqué template on page 71.

A star is the background for the Honey Bee Star Painted Appliqué project. Instructions for the Star Painted Appliqué are on page 78.

Prepare the templates and the appliqué pieces according to the Painted Appliqué Technique 1 described on page 14. The Honey Bee is traced as one unit.

Step :

1 Use a black fabric marker to color the stripes on the body and the head. Use a blue Sanford Colorific Gel Marker to color the top of the head and the stripe. Also, make little dots on the black stripes as shown in the photo.

2 Use a yellow Sanford Colorfic Gel Marker to color the two stripes on the body. Use an orange Sanford Colorfic Gel Marker to make little dots on the yellow.

3 Mix together one part PaintFusion and one part Dry Pigment Paint by LuminArte, PE – 144 Dragonfly Wing. For a stronger color, add more dry pigment. Paint both wings. Let dry.

4 Use three different colored Gelly Roll markers to carefully dot the wings.

5 Mix 3 tablespoons of Liquitex Yellow Medium with ⅛ teaspoon of Dry Pigment Paint by LuminArte PE – 156 French Vanilla. Mix well. Paint each hexagon.

6 Use the black marker to dot the outer edges of the hexagons.

7 Glue the Honey Bee and Hexagons to the Star Appliqué and appliqué together.

8 To make the circular background, refer to pages 17–18 or glue the appliqué to the background of your choice.

Finishing
Step :

1 Trim the background fabric from behind the appliqués and remove the freezer paper or fusible water-soluble stabilizer as directed on page 13.

2 Trim the background to 20½" x 20½". Add borders as desired.

Painted Appliqué

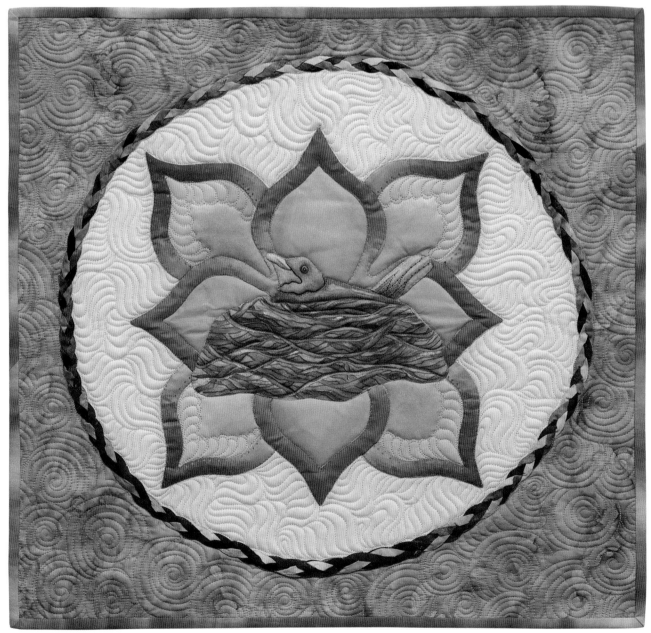

Mama Bird Star

20" x 20"

Size of appliquéd center panel: 16" x 16"

Designed, painted, and machine appliquéd by Linda M. Poole. Machine quilted by Lisa Sipes, Philadelphia, Pennsylvania.

Fabric Requirements

Background: 21½" x 21½" square of blue
  17½" x 17½" square of a light color

Appliqué: ½ yard PFD or white, tightly woven
  100% cotton

Art Supplies

Derwent Water-Soluble Ink Pencils:
  Chili Red, Sun Yellow, Tangerine, Fuchsia,
  Sea Blue, Teal Green, Violet, and
  many different browns

InkFusion Fabric Medium

Use the Mama Bird Appliqué template on pages 74–76.

A star is the background for the Mama Bird Star Painted Appliqué project. Instructions for the Star Painted Appliqué are on page 78.

Prepare the templates and the appliqué pieces according to the Painted Appliqué Technique 1 described on page 14.

Step :

1 Trace the bird and nest as one piece.

2 With a pencil, lightly draw pairs of lines as if you were drawing twigs. Weave your double lines over and under one another.

3 Firmly color all the twigs using different colors of brown Derwent Inktense pencils. Use Chile Red in some of the areas to give the illusion of depth. Make more browns by blending colors.

Tip : If you do not want to draw twigs and color them individually, you can paint random lines with textile paints of different browns to make the twigs.

4 Firmly color the bird beak with Sun Yellow. Lightly outline the beak and accent the bottom with Tangerine.

Firmly color the top of the head with Sea Blue. Firmly color under the beak with Teal Green. Firmly color the upper back of the bird with Fuchsia. Firmly color the rest of the bird's back with Violet.

Firmly color the tail feathers with Teal Green. Color the base of the tail near the bird's back with Sea Blue.

5 Dip a small paintbrush into InkFusion, putting just a tad onto the brush, and paint over the colored areas. Be sure to clean your brush before going to a new color.

6 Trim the excess fabric and complete the appliqué as directed in the basic technique.

7 Glue the Mama Bird and Nest to the Star Appliqué and appliqué together.

8 To make the circular background, refer to pages 17–18 or glue the appliqué to the background of your choice.

Finishing

Step :

1 Trim the background fabric from behind the appliqués and remove the freezer paper or fusible water-soluble stabilizer as directed on page 13.

2 Trim the background to 20½" x 20½". Add borders as desired.

Appliqué

Fancy Heart

25" x 27"

Size of appliquéd center panel: 18½" x 20½"

Designed and machine appliquéd by Linda M. Poole. Machine quilted by Karen McTavish, Hayward, Wisconsin.

Fabric Requirements

Background: 20" x 22" rectangle of a light color

Leaves: 1 fat quarter each of light, medium, and dark green

Flowers: Large scraps of light, medium, and dark pink

Swirls: Large scraps

Bias Tape: 32" of green bias tape

Use the Fancy Heart templates on pages 95–96.

Prepare the templates and the appliqué pieces according to the Glue Stick Appliqué Technique described on pages 11–13.

Tip : There is no piece between 22L and 23L and no piece between 22R and 23R. The red lines are used only in the painted version of Fancy Heart.

Step :

1 Glue 8L to 8R. Appliqué together.

2 Glue pieces 19L and 19R to piece 18. Appliqué together.

3 Glue 1L and 6L to 5L. Appliqué together. Glue 1R and 6R to 5R. Appliqué together.

4 Glue 12L to 13L to 14L to 15L to 16L to make a flower. Appliqué together. Repeat with pieces 12R through 16R.

5 Glue 11L to the appropriate flower. Repeat with 11R. Appliqué together.

6 Glue 26L to 27 to 26R. Glue 23L to 25L.

Glue 23R to 25R.

Glue 21L to 22L.

Glue 21R to 22R. Appliqué all the glued areas.

7 Glue unit 23L-25L to unit 26L-27-26R. Glue unit 23R -25R to the opposite side of unit 26L-27-26R.

8 Glue 24L and 24R to the appliquéd unit from directly above. Appliqué together.

9 Glue units 21L-25L and 21R-25R to the appliquéd unit. Appliqué together.

10 Glue 20 to the center flower. Appliqué together.

11 Glue 1L-5L-6L to piece 9L. Repeat with unit 1R-5R-6R and piece 9R. Appliqué the glued areas.

12 Glue units 1L-5L-6L-9L and 1R-5R-6R-9R to the background fabric.

13 Apply glue to the back of the bias tape or use fusible bias tape. Lift up areas where you need to tuck the seam allowances of the bias tape under another piece. Glue or iron the bias tape in place. Appliqué the bias tape and units to the background fabric.

14 Glue on the center flower unit by gently lifting up bias tape. Appliqué the bias tape and flower unit to the background fabric.

15 Glue the smaller flowers on top of the bias tape seam allowance. Appliqué.

16 Glue unit 17L-17R over the seam allowances of bias tape and piece 20. Glue unit 19L-18-19R to the background, gently lifting the bottom of 17R and placing it on top of unit 19L-18-19R. Appliqué.

17 Glue 2L, 3L, 4L, 2R, 3R, 4R, 7L, 8L, 7R, 8R, and 10 to the background. Appliqué.

Finishing

Step :

1 Trim the background fabric from behind the appliqués and remove the freezer paper or fusible water-soluable stabilizer as directed on page 13.

2 Trim the background to 19" x 21". Add borders as desired.

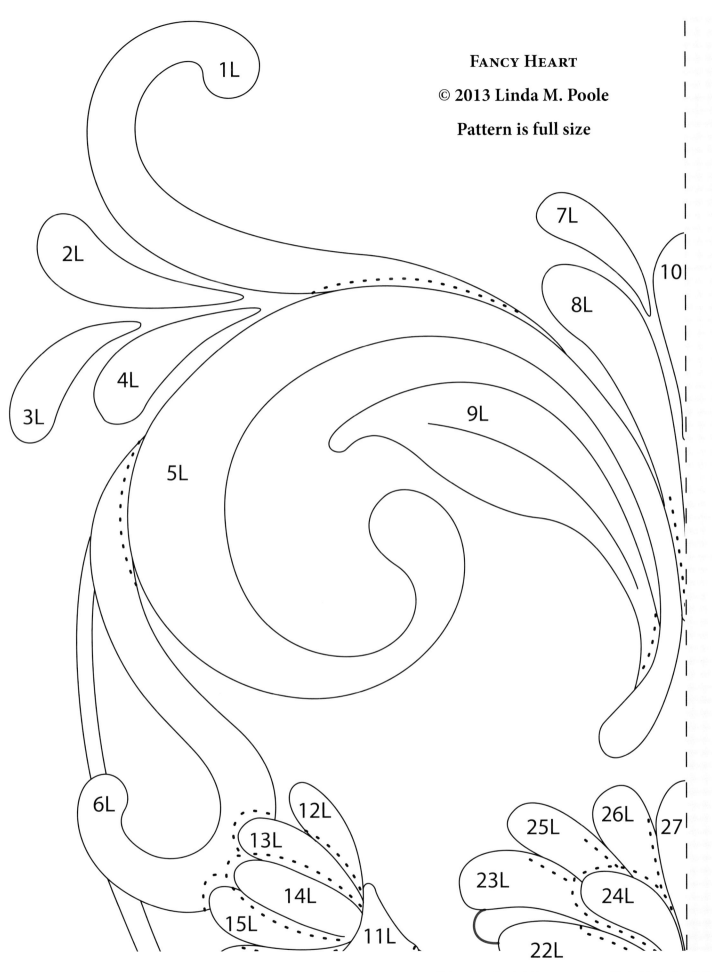

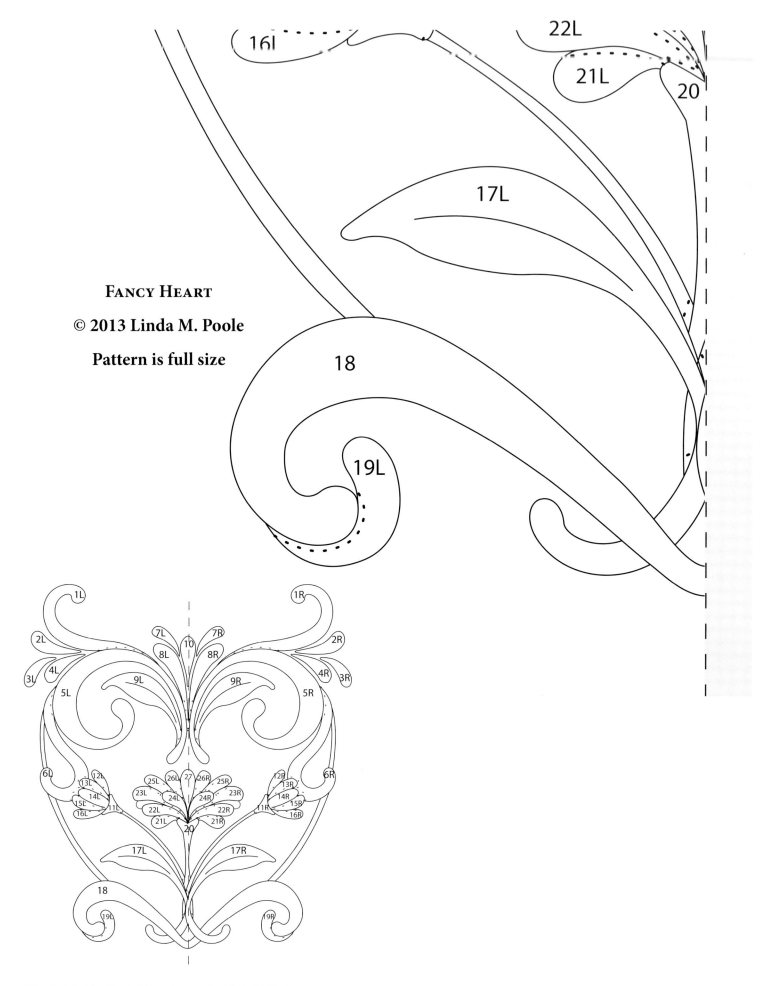

Fancy Heart

© 2013 Linda M. Poole

Pattern is full size

Painted Appliqué

Fancy Heart

25½" x 27"

Size of appliquéd center panel: 17" x 18"

Designed, painted, machine appliquéd, and quilted by Linda M. Poole

Fabric Requirements

Background: 18½" x 19½" rectangle of a light color

Swirls, Flowers, and Leaves: ½ yard PFD or
white, tightly woven 100% cotton

Bias Tape: 32" of green bias tape

Art Supplies

InkFusion Fabric Medium

Derwent Inktense Water-Soluble Ink Pencils:
Field Green, Violet, Sea Blue, Teal Green,
and Apple Green

Use the Fancy Heart templates on pages 95–96.

Prepare the PFD or white cotton fabric and templates according to the Painted Appliqué Technique 1 as described on page 14.

Step :

1 Using Violet InkTense, firmly color the bottom sections of each petal (12L through 16L and 12R through 16R).

2 Color the tops of each petal with Sea Blue. Blend the Sea Blue into the Violet. Press firmly and outline the edges of each petal with Sea Blue.

Color 11L and 11R with Field Green. Press firmly when coloring the top and sides. Remember, the harder you press, the more intense the color becomes.

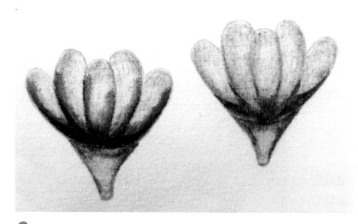

3 Dip a small paintbrush into InkFusion, putting just a tad onto the brush, and paint over each petal and the green areas.

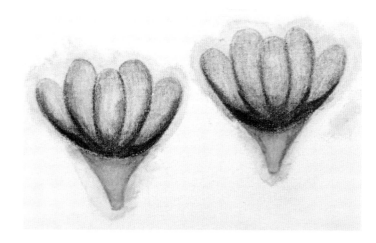

4 Pressing firmly, color the bottom center of 19L-18-19R with Teal Green. Pressing firmly, outline 19 with Teal Green and color where 19 meets 18.

5 Color the remainder of 19 with Teal Green. From the center of 18, color outwards with Teal Green, but do not press as firmly as before.

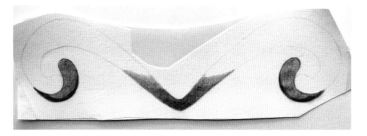

6 Continue coloring as shown with Field Green.

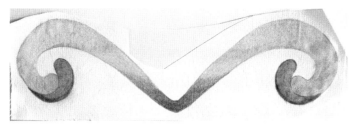

7 Continue coloring as shown with Apple Green.

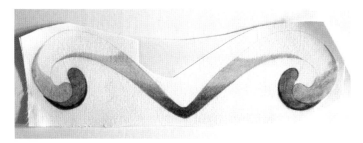

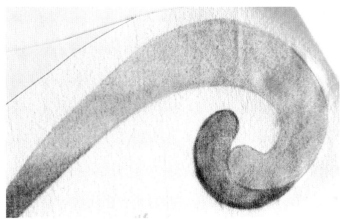

8 Dip a medium size paintbrush into InkFusion. Start in the center and paint outward. Paint 19. Be sure to paint outside the traced lines.

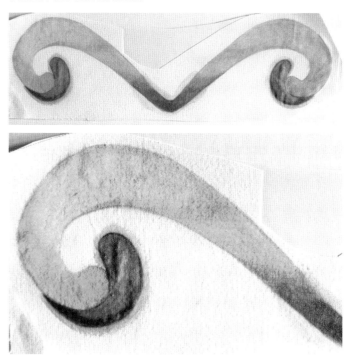

9 Starting from the center and moving outward and upward, paint 18 with InkFusion. Be sure to blend well where two colors meet.

10 Press firmly and color the bottom of each petal of the center flower with Violet and lightly color upward.

11 Color the rest of the petals with Sea Blue. Press firmer toward the top of each petal.

12 Dip a paintbrush into InkFusion. Start in the center and paint upward. Make sure you paint outside the traced lines.

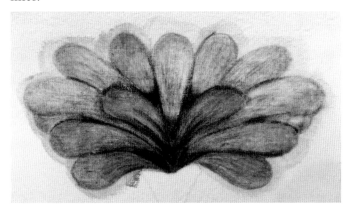

13 Color the stem with Field Green and the top portion with Teal Green. Dip a paintbrush into InkFusion and paint the colored areas. Make sure you paint outside the drawn lines.

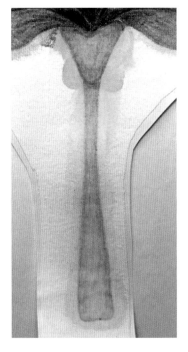

14 Color the bottom and stem portions of 17L and 17R with Teal Green. Color the stem area of 17R using firm pressure. Color the tops of 17L and 17R with Field Green.

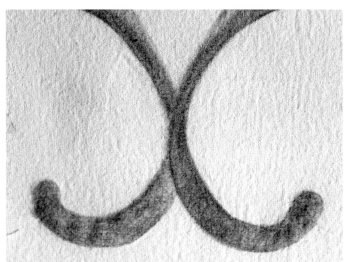

15 Dip a paintbrush into InkFusion and paint the colored areas. Make sure you paint outside the drawn lines.

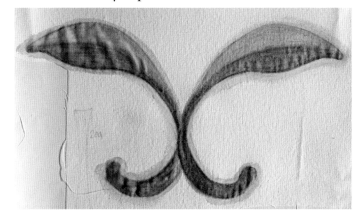

16 Color the following pieces as directed on page 101: 7L, 7R, 10, 2L, 2R, 3L, 3R, 4L, 4R, 8L, and 8R.

Color the bottom of each section with Teal Green. Color the top of each section with Field Green. Be sure to blend the two colors where they meet.

Color the lighter areas of each section with Field Green. Be sure to blend the two colors where they meet.

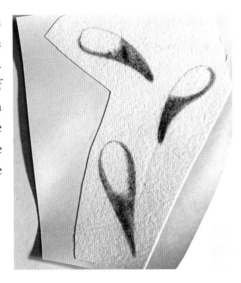

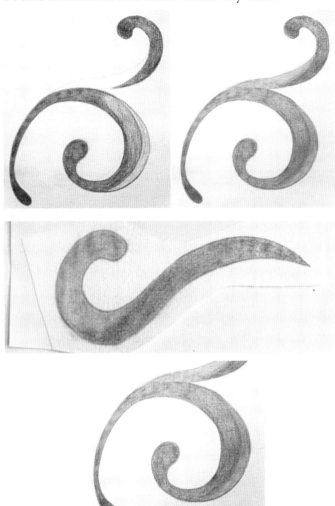

17 Dip a paintbrush into InkFusion and paint the colored areas. Make sure you paint outside the drawn lines.

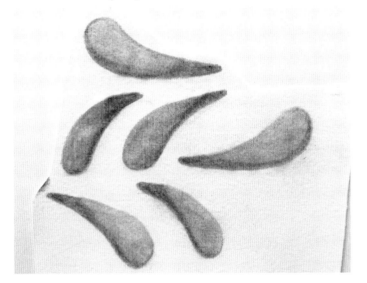

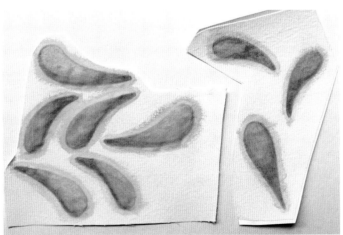

18 To paint units 1L-5L-6L and 1R-5R-6R, color the darker areas in the photo of each section with Teal Green.

19 Dip a paintbrush into InkFusion and paint the colored areas. Make sure you paint outside the drawn lines.

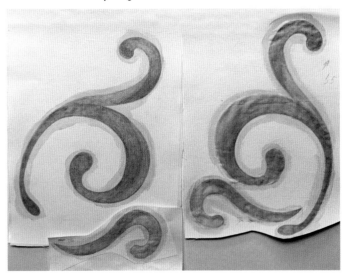

20 Color the bottom of pieces 9 and 9R with Teal Green. Color the top area with Field Green. Be sure to blend the two colors where they meet.

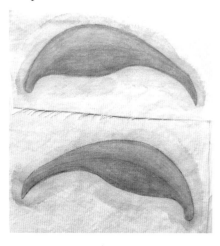

Dip a paintbrush into InkFusion and paint the colored areas. Make sure you paint outside the drawn lines.

21 Glue or fuse the bias tape for the sides of the heart onto the background fabric. Appliqué.

Glue 1L-5L-6L to 8L to 9L. Appliqué together.

Glue the unit over the bias tape seam allowances. Appliqué the unit to the background fabric.

Repeat with pieces 1R-5R-6R, 8R, and 9R.

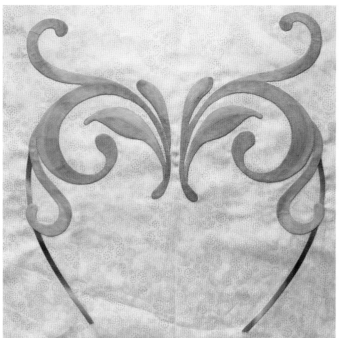

22 Glue 2L, 3L, 4L, 2R, 3R, 4R, 7L, 7R, and 10 to the background. Appliqué.

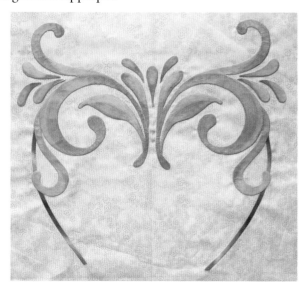

23 Glue or iron the bias tape stems to the background fabric. Glue the center flower/stem unit in place by gently lifting up the bias tape. Appliqué the bias tape and flower segment to the background fabric.

24 Glue both smaller flowers on top of the bias tape seam allowance. Appliqué.

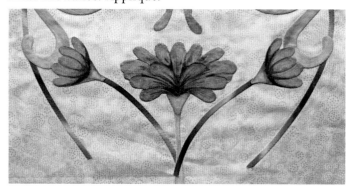

25 Glue unit 18-19 to 17L and 17R by gently lifting the bottom of 17R and placing the right side of unit 18-19 underneath. Appliqué together.

26 Glue and appliqué unit 18-19-17L-17R to the background.

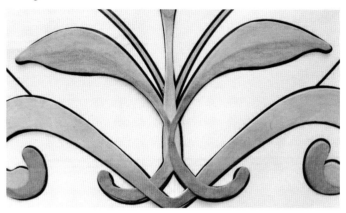

Finishing

Step :

1 Trim the background fabric from behind the appliqués and remove the freezer paper or fusible water-soluble stabilizer as directed on page 13.

2 Trim the background to 17½" x 18½". Add borders as desired.

3 Add beads or gems, if desired.

Appliqué

Ring Around the Posies

25½" x 26½"

Size of appliquéd center panel: 18½" x 19½"

Designed, painted, and machine quilted by Linda M. Poole.
Hand appliquéd by Gloria Grohs, Leesburg, Florida.

Fabric Requirements

Background: 20" x 21" rectangle of a light color

Swirls and Leaves: two fat quarters of different greens

Flowers: large scraps or fat quarters

Prepare the templates and the appliqué pieces according to the Glue Stick Appliqué Technique described on pages 11–13.

Use the RING AROUND THE POSIES template on page 106. For this project, disregard the red lines on the template.

Step :

1 Glue A1 to A2 to A3 to A4 to A5 to A6. Glue A to the center to complete an A flower. Appliqué together. Make seven A flowers.

2 Glue B1 to B2 to B3 to B4 to B5 to B6. Glue B to the center to complete a B flower. Appliqué together. Make three B flowers.

3 Glue C1 to C2 to C3 to C4 to C5 to C6. Glue an A flower to the center of the C flower.

4 Appliqué together.

5 Glue D to an A flower. Appliqué together. Repeat adding DR, E, and ER to the remaining three A flowers. Refer to the pattern illustration for more details.

6 Glue G and GR to unit A-C. Appliqué together.

7 Glue F1 to F2 to F3. Appliqué together. Repeat to make units F1R-F2R-F3R, G1-G2-G3, and G1R-G2R-G3R.

8 Glue unit F1-F2-F3 to one Flower A to unit A-C-G to another Flower A to unit F1R-F2R-F3R. Appliqué together.

9 Glue A-D to unit G1-G2-G3. Glue A-ER to unit G1R-G2R-G3R. Appliqué the glued areas.

10 Glue all units to background fabric. Appliqué.

Finishing
Step :

1 Trim the background fabric from behind the appliqués and remove the freezer paper or fusible water-soluble stabilizer as directed on page 13.

2 Trim the background to 19" x 20". Add borders as desired.

RING AROUND THE POSIES

© **2013 Linda M. Poole**

Enlarge pattern 200%

Painted Appliqué

Ring Around the Posies

21" x 23"

Size of appliquéd center panel: 17½" x 19½"

Designed, painted, machine appliquéd by Linda M. Poole. Machine quilted by Pamela Joy Dransfeldt, Camarillo, California.

Fabric Requirements

Background: 19" x 21" rectangle of a light color

Small Flowers: ½ yard PFD or white, tightly woven
   100% cotton

Swirls: Scraps of assorted greens

Large flower: Large scrap of yellow

Art Supplies

InkFusion Fabric Medium

Derwent Inktense Water-Soluble Ink Pencils:
   Fuchsia, Yellow, Green, Lavender, and
   other colors of your choice

The A and B flowers are painted in this pattern. All other pieces are traditional appliqué. Prepare the PFD or white cotton fabric and templates for the A and B flowers according to the Painted Appliqué Technique 2 as described on pages 15–16.

Use the RING AROUND THE POSIES template on page 106.

Prepare the templates and the appliqué pieces for all remaining pieces according to the Glue Stick Appliqué Technique described on pages 11–13.

Paint the seven A flowers as directed below.

Step:

1 Firmly outline the star with a green Derwent Inktense pencil.

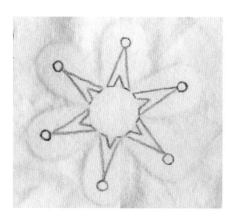

2 Firmly color the circles and inside the star shape. The circles can be different colors for each flower if you choose. Use a darker shade of green to color the wider area of the star points.

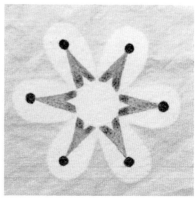

3 Firmly color the center of the flower with yellow. Firmly color the point in the center of the green area with orange. Lightly color a little circle of orange inside the center of the yellow circle.

4 Firmly color the flower petals with fuchsia. Press harder on the insides of the petals.

5 Dip a small paintbrush into InkFusion, putting just a tad onto the brush, and paint over the orange points. Drag the brush toward the yellow center circle.

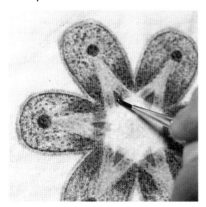

6 Dip a small paintbrush into InkFusion, putting just a tad onto the brush, and paint over the dark green areas. Drag the color up and into the lighter green to blend.

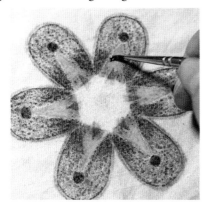

7 Dip a paintbrush into InkFusion and paint the dark areas of fuchsia, dragging up and into the lighter colored fuchsia areas to blend.

8 Paint three B flowers, omitting the outer star points.

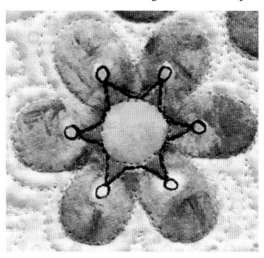

9 Follow the instructions for the traditional appliqué RING AROUND THE POSIES to complete the appliquéd project.

Finishing

Step :

1 Trim the background from behind the appliqués. Remove the freezer paper or fusible water-soluble stabilizer as directed on page 13.

2 Trim the background to 18" x 20". Add borders as desired.

Resources

Let us keep our Quilt Shops in business and support them in every way possible!

Linda M. Poole
Milford, PA
Lectures/Workshops
www.lindampoole
e-mail: Linda@lindampoole.com
Check for added products at her store.

Cotton & Monofilament Threads
Aurifil™
http://www.aurifil.com
Established in 1983, Aurifil is an accomplished Italian company based in Milano, with experience in producing superior quality cotton threads for professional and domestic quilters.
*Found in quilt shops or online

Superior Threads®
www.superiorthreads.com
Superior Threads began in 1998 as an at-home business by husband-and-wife duo, Bob and Heather Purcell. Superior Threads started out of the Purcell's garage, and now spans over a 25,000 sq/ft facility in the red rocks of St. George, Utah.
*Found in quilt shops or online

Basting Spray
KK2000™ Temporary Adhesive Spray
Sulky®
http://www.sulky.com
Contains up to 70% more usable product because it is made of a highly concentrated material combined with a low-pressure spray that eliminates wasteful over spraying.

Paint, Brushes & Art Supplies
Dick Blick
http://www.dickblick.com/

Pro Chemical and Dye®
http://www.prochemicalanddye.com

Dharma Trading
http://www.dharmatrading.com/

Jerry's Artarama
http://www.jerrysartarama.com

Joggles
http://www.joggles.com

Specialty Paint Medium
InkFusion™, PaintFusion™
Sherry Rogers-Harrison
www.Sewfarsewgood.org
sewfarsewgood@comcast.com
206-412-4720

Dry Pigment
LuminArte
http://www.dreamingcolor.com
Primary Elements Artist Pigments™
Jacquard Pearl Ex Powdered Pigments
http://www.jacquardproducts.com

Freezer Paper
C. Jenkins Co.
C. Jenkins 8.5" x 11" Freezer Paper Sheets (50 Sheets)
http://www.cjenkinscompany.com

Reynolds® Freezer Paper
Found in grocery stores

Water Soluble Stabilizer Sheets
Floriani Stitch N Wash Fusible®
Comes in 8.5" x 11" sheets, 12" x 10 yards, 12" x 25 yards, and 20" x 10 yards

RNK Distributing
http://www.rnkdistributing.com

I Have a Notion
http://ihavea-notion.com

Red Rock Threads
http://www.redrockthreads.com

Wash-Away Appliqué Sheets
www.lindampoole.com

Longarm Services
Pamela Joy Dransfeldt,
Joyful Quilter
PJQuilt7@aol.com
http://joyfulquiltermachinequilting.com/

Karen McTavish
McTavish Quilting Studio
Hayward, Wisconsin
Kmctavish@designerquilts.com
www.designerquilts.com

Lisa Sipes
Http://thatcrazyquiltygirl.
blogspot.com
Lmms1981@gmail.com

PFD (Prepared for Dyeing) Fabric
Soft Expressions
http://www.softexpressions.com

Dharma Trading
http://www.dharmatrading.com/

Clover® Fusible Bias Tape Makers
Linda M. Poole
www.lindampoole.com

Fabric
eQuilter
www.equilter.com

Lightweight Fusible Interfacing
Pellon®
www.pellon.com

Lighting
Stella Lighting
Stella's easy touch interface allows you to turn on/off, dim up or down, and change light spectrum all with a quick, light touch.
http://stellalighting.com/

Batting
Warm and Natural®
The Warm™ Company
www.warmcompany.com

About the Author

Photograph by Bonnie McCaffery, Hawley, Pennsylvania, www.bonniemccaffery.com

When I was a little girl, I had an insatiable desire to make things. Luckily, I come from a family that understood me all too well. My roots have been firmly planted by a talented, loving, generous European family that always put family first and strongly encouraged freedom of artistic expression. I have inherited the good fortune of learning from generations of artists, silversmiths, sculptors, poets, weavers, stained glass artisans, and writers.

My maternal grandmother let me work the treadle part of the sewing machine while she sewed. My grandmother was a smart cookie. She found a way of giving an energetic little girl a way to have fun and participate. Soon, she propped me on her lap and showed me how to sew.

I had my own needles, scissors, and threads before kindergarten and was taught to respect my tools. I remember my mother teaching me to crochet, knit, and embroider. My father took me on adventures. I always had my little Instamatic camera in tow. My Christmas gifts were always about art, sewing, and creating. An artist's easel, paints, brushes, paper, and my own art table were some of my favorite gifts. As an adult looking back, I am thankful for the thought and time my parents gave to nurturing my curiosity and love for art.

My whole life has always revolved around photography, writing, painting, and sewing. These interests have fueled my passion for travel, teaching, and sharing my experiences with people around the world. I have taught throughout the United States, the United Kingdom, Germany, Turkey, and Italy. I believe language is never a barrier in the translation of quilts.

Let the things you see in my book be a springboard for your imagination. Each pattern gives you choices—use commercial fabrics, paint your fabric, or do both!

Linda

Linda Poole lives with her husband, Ray Williams, and Corgi pup, Zoie, near Milford, Pennsylvania, a beautiful region in the northeastern part of the state. Together they share the passion of discovering the gifts of nature while hiking trails that lead to creeks, brooks, rivers, and lakes. Ray can be found with his fishing pole in hand with Linda by his side, clicking away with her camera.

More AQS Books

This is only a small selection of the books available from the American Quilter's Society. AQS books are known worldwide for timely topics, clear writing, beautiful color photos, and accurate illustrations and patterns. The following books are available from your local bookseller, quilt shop, or public library.

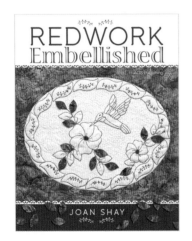

#1422

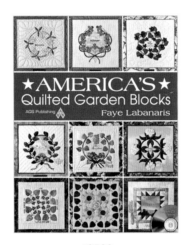

#8530

#8347

#8664

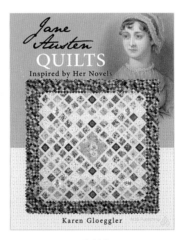

#1415

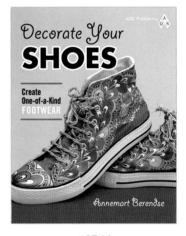

#8766

#8665

#1417

#1423

LOOK for these books nationally.
CALL or **VISIT** our website at

1-800-626-5420
www.AmericanQuilter.com